# INCENTIVES *and* PLANNING
## *in* SOCIAL POLICY

# INCENTIVES *and* PLANNING
## *in* SOCIAL POLICY

*Edited by* BRUNO STEIN *and* S. M. MILLER

*New York University*

ALDINE PUBLISHING COMPANY/*Chicago*

First published 1973 by
Aldine Publishing Company
529 South Wabash Avenue
Chicago, Illinois 60605

ISBN 0-202-06058-6
Library of Congress Catalog Number 72-92841

Printed in the United States of America

# Contents

# Preface

This collection of essays is the outcome of a unique project conducted at New York University and supported by the U.S. Department of Health, Education and Welfare. Entitled "Working Parties in Social Policy Analysis," the project, initiated by Lewis Butler, Assistant Secretary for Planning and Evaluation, DHEW, sought to stimulate academic research on social policy questions with particular emphasis on the information needs of government policy makers. The topics for the project were jointly decided upon by NYU and by a group, headed by James G. Abert, Jr. The individual projects that emerged from this decision were then sponsored by NYU. Responsibility for the selection of researchers and for monitoring the projects rested with us rather than with DHEW.

Publication of the total output from the project was not feasible, since this involved over a dozen long and somewhat technical research reports, some over a hundred pages in length. However, we believed that students of social policy would benefit from a set of essays that illustrate the scope and method of social research today. With this in mind, we selected parts of six of the projects, basing our choice on the criteria of topicality, a more or less common theme of incentives and planning, and a distribution of subject matter among health, education, and welfare.

A complete list of acknowledgments would be far too lengthy to print. Dozens of scholars around the country gave advice and help in the selection of researchers, the choice of topics, and the design of some of the projects. Our thanks to all of them, as well as to the group at ASPE with whom we worked and from whom we learned, and to Dr. Laurence E. Lynn, Jr., who made this volume possible. At NYU we owe a debt of gratitude to Ed Enroth, Lou Scesa, and Jim Smith for coping with the administrative snarls that the project produced for them, as well as to Leslie Blachman, Judy Brewin, and Marsha Kroll. Extra special thanks go to Judith A. Stein for expert editorial help.

The material in this project was prepared under contract number HEW-OS-69-94. Researchers undertaking projects under government sponsorship are encouraged to express freely their professional judgment. Therefore, points of view stated herein do not necessarily represent the official position or policy of the Department of Health, Education and Welfare.

# INCENTIVES *and* PLANNING *in* SOCIAL POLICY

# I

## Introduction

Bruno Stein *is professor of economics at New York University, the institution from which he holds the B.A., M.A., and Ph.D. in economics. With a research and teaching interest in labor and social economics, he has published extensively on labor problems, manpower, and on the economics of public assistance. The focus of his work has been on income distribution and the conflicts it engenders. With respect to the latter, he also serves as arbitrator, mediator, and fact-finder in labor disputes, on call from the panels of the American Arbitration Association and the New York Public Employment Relations Board. Dr. Stein is the author of* On Relief: The Economics of Poverty and Public Welfare.

# Incentives and Planning as Social Policy Tools

## BRUNO STEIN

Social policy is emerging as a new and separate field of study, separate, that is, from the traditional social sciences. However, both theory and practice in social policy are as old as time. Social policy has been made by governments since the year one and analyzed since the year two. The novelty that we currently perceive comes from the end of the myth of *laissez-faire* (a myth that bemused this country for about one hundred years), and from the consequent realization that social stability requires that "social problems" either need to be ameliorated or, at least, appear to be in the process of solution. The ideology of *laissez-faire* had allowed governments to treat economic and social problems as acts of the market place or, what was much the same thing, as acts of God. As a religion, *laissez-faire* left plenty of scope for sinning. Yet, in spite of the fact that all levels of government intervened incessantly in economic and social matters during the 19th and early 20th centuries, the belief persisted that governments could not and should not try to cure social ills. The "could" was more important than the "should", since it was widely believed that intervention made things worse rather than better.

Depression and war relaxed our inhibitions against intervention, while the economic growth and social development of the United States after World War II generated acute social

3

problems. By the 1960's there existed a generation of voters who assumed that legislative bodies were paid to solve problems. The voters of the 1970's will find any other viewpoint rather quaint. It is an error to consider this activist mood as a triumph of liberals over conservatives, or Democrats over Republicans. It is merely an adaption to the needs of a large and crowded and urbanized industrial society.

The decline of *laissez-faire* has made social policy-making not only respectable but an overt and normal form of government behavior. If it is going to be pursued as a regular government activity, it might as well be done efficiently and effectively. Accordingly, a labor market has developed for people who claim skills in social policy matters.

In short, what was once done as a sideline (or practiced under another rubric) is being done professionally. A profession implies—indeed nowadays it requires—expertise and the blessings of a graduate university degree; hence, a new field of study which involved many specialists other than economists. But with the rise of social welfare and education expenditures in the sixties, economists again spread their diagrams and equations into the field of social policy. Their objectives were to provide tools for making choices (as in cost-benefit analysis) and a mode of constructing and analyzing organizations and institutions (as in planning-programming-budgeting systems).

If economics was once "the dismal science," so social policy analysis emerges as the optimistic social science. It presupposes that problems can be solved, or at least alleviated. True, social policy has limits in that many of our problems are caused by the political and social institutions that dominate our lives or, worse yet, by some intractable human nature that makes us greedy, aggressive, and non-cooperative. These limits form the boundary within which social policy can function. Common sense tells us, for example, that a hospital can be run badly or well; by extension, it is possible to improve a poor regional health delivery system. Systematic knowledge can be applied to improve the performance of specified social institutions. Aspects of life *can* be improved.

Knowledge alone does not suffice. In a world of scarce resources, a social policy uses some of these resources, reallocating them from their alternative uses. It is almost impossible to reallocate resources without redistributing income. Accordingly, a policy is likely to impose costs on some and benefits on others. A Pareto-optimal policy—one that makes someone better off without making anyone worse off—is best reserved for economic theory textbooks. However, the concept suggests the following normative proposition: if a given policy goal can be achieved economically or wastefully, then the economical solution is the preferable one.

The introduction of an efficiency criterion brings economic thinking into play. Good economic thinking (please note the qualifier) uses a human failing, namely greed, to accomplish desirable human ends. Good economic thinking is also systematic, because training in economic theory is, if nothing else, training in logic. But these advantages are purchased at a price. Economists tend to view social problems with a detachment that can be inhuman. A hard nose may not be a much better attribute for social planning than a fat head. The element of compassion is needed for a process that seeks to improve human life.

The studies in this volume deal with incentives and planning, and thus reveal the inroads that economic thinking has made on social policy. A number of the authors are economists, but not all of them by any means. Just as a war is too important to be left to generals, so are questions of incentives too important to be left to economists. An incentive is something that induces one to take action or work harder; it is the stimulus part of a stimulus-response mechanism. Psychologists may devote large amounts of research to this topic, yet economists (with some exceptions) remain unaware of the complexities involved. The economic view of human behavior is that a person is made happier with more goods and services (or with the money to buy them), subject to diminishing marginal utility for any one good. Hence, behavior can be altered by some offer of money that is great enough to overcome the unhappiness connected with any change in behavior. This is not a bad first approximation of market behavior but, on close examination, the economic theory of incentives is either too simplistic to predict behavior that involves non-pecuniary cost and gratifications, or so tautological that it does not predict at all. To leave incentives and planning studies solely in the hands of economists is to leave the social honey pot in the hands of the bears. The bears' satisfaction will be maximized, all right, but at the expense of the community.

This is especially important when responses to economic stimuli are, *a priori*, likely to be complex. For example, revenue-sharing is a political device whose intellectual champions have tended to be economists of both liberal and conservative varieties. The hypothesis of revenue-sharing is that when relatively unrestricted funds are made available to state (or local) agencies, these agencies would have an incentive to redevelop their planning mechanisms in order to solve problems in their own, imaginative ways. But, as Cohen and McCann demonstrate, the experience from Title I of the Elementary and Secondary Act shows that the financial stimulus does not bring about the desired response.

The Cohen and McCann study of the Title I ESEA experience brings political science and history to bear on a federal policy that once held hope for improving the education of underprivileged children. What is important about their findings is not that the policy was not especially successful—this has been established by others—but that the revenue-sharing or block grant *method* is not a device for strengthening weak levels of government. Despite its lack of success, revenue-sharing remains a widely touted specific for many social ailments. The policy analysts, in this instance found it useful to scrutinize not merely the policy but the *method*, *i.e.* the vehicle for the policy. This includes administrative details that, although frequently sloughed aside in the literature, contain the vital elements of the policy.

Dissatisfaction with the state of education has led to various proposals to pay teachers (or other educational contractors) on the basis of the quality of the service rendered. Better pay for better service is an incentive to deliver better service.

Furthermore, it has elements of distributive justice about it. Everyone has either had an incompetent teacher or known one. The oral and written tradition is rich in anecdotes about teachers who can't teach Johnny to read. All educational incentive proposals that have recently been in vogue, including performance contracting to extramural firms, assume that a desired goal can be quantified, *e.g.*, that achievement tests serve as satisfactory measures of policy goals. The proposals further assume that different behavior by teachers, and different methods, not only lead to the desired score changes but do so without causing deleterious side-effects.

Within the scope of such assumptions, Bellin and Bellin lay out the issues involved in adapting the performance-contracting concept to public schools. How will teachers perceive a revised reward system, both as individuals and as organized professionals? What risks does such a system present to administrators? Whereas economists tend to view incentives as something to which individuals respond, the Bellins wisely couch their analysis in terms of group or organizational behavior. This enables them to deal with selected issues such as 1) who, besides teachers, should receive incentives, 2) whether group or individual incentives are more effective, 3) the use of discretionary funds, and 4) methods of calculating bonus pay. There is no magic in incentive pay for teachers. The Bellins treat it as a possibly useful first step toward educational change, but warn that by itself it offers limited prospect for success. Among other measures, they call for massive federal fiscal support of schools and for the development of an effective parent constituency.

When we turn to the first of the studies done by economists, we see the "hard" approach that is characteristic of modern economics, and that is often so offensive to non-economists. Yet the Singell and Yordon study is an excellent piece of work, a good example of the directions that social policy research will turn to if it wishes to ground itself in social *science*. The Singell and Yordon paper seeks to "develop a testable model for achieving efficiency in public education." It is one of several possible models that rely on cash, but the writers do not insist that cash is necessarily preferable to other incentives. In short, instead of searching for one unique solution to educational problems, Singell and Yordon pursue a given line of inquiry from idea to research design. Assuming a policy goal of improving educational output as measured by achievement scores, Singell and Yordon address themselves to the question: what would make a difference? Their critical review of the literature convinces them that existing studies of the determinants of pupil performance are at too high a level of aggregation for variables other than social class to make much difference; worse yet, most studies are cross-sectional, a method that obscures the effect of events that occurred in earlier grades. Accordingly, Singell and Yordon conducted a longitudinal study in a particular school district designed to relate individual pupil achievement scores to specific differences in teacher input, social status of pupils, and a rough (and admittedly weak) measure of pupils' innate endowments.

The study yields six propositions regarding 1) the educational system's responsiveness to higher- and lower-achieving students, 2) the use of reading scores as surrogate measures of achievement, 3) the influence of teachers' ages on educational outcomes, 4) the learning handicap imposed on the student from the poor family when he attends a school with other poor children, 5) the characteristics of first-grade teachers that are predictors of student's later achievement, and 6) the question of cultural bias in testing devices. On the basis of these six propositions, Singell and Yordon drew up a proposal for an experimental program to improve the academic performance for first-grade children with low reading-readiness scores. The proposal provides incentives to middle-class schools to accept lower-class pupils; it also suggests an economic incentive to government to engage in such experimentation.

Health promises to be one of the great social policy issues of the 1970's. Rising pressure for more and better health services is forcing the re-examination of traditional ways of doing business in health. The pressure manifests itself in ever higher prices for health services, and it leads to a search for more efficient allocation of the existing supply of health resources as well as to ways to increase the total supply. Here is where much planning needs to be done. Unfortunately, local health officials honor the planning process in the breach rather than in the observance. One reason for this may be that local health officials have experience in managing their own separate facilities, but little knowledge of how to coordinate the activities of various independent health facilities—some public, some voluntay, and some proprietary. John Moore's paper is an example of the contributions that can come from yet another social science—management science. Effective planning means effective resource management, and Moore shows how to translate the planning talk into planning action.

While Moore deals with the more efficient use of local health resources, Lave, Lave, and Morton look for ways of altering the mix of resources in the physician's office. The basic problem is the apparent shortage and maldistribution of physicians. One approach to this problem is to increase the number and functions of paramedical personnel. Lave *et al.* have surveyed the present state of knowledge on paramedics. They concluded that programs to train and use such personnel have much to offer as a partial solution to the doctor shortage.

The relief of poverty must be the oldest task for social policy. By tradition, the poor have been divided into two categories; the impotent poor and the able-bodied ones. Help for the former may be a matter for social conscience and public generosity, but incentives enter into the question of helping the poor who are at work and those who, in some sense, could be at work. In the United States in the early seventies, this issue has become especially acute. It is widely believed that the availability of public assistance constitutes a major disincentive to work. Hence, reform proposals take two shapes: programs to force the able-bodied poor into the labor market or into work-relief projects ("workfare") and programs to make work financially more attractive by the use of negative tax-type welfare payments.

Rein takes up the question from a comparative viewpoint. He shows that incentives are far less of a preoccupation in the income-maintenance systems of other industrial countries.

The problem of high welfare benefits and their attendent disincentives is the obverse of the problem of low wages. Indeed rising welfare benefits are one way in which a society discovers, and comes to recognize, its low-wage sector. This suggests that the real problem of incentives among the able-bodied poor may be the lack of jobs at non-poverty wages. The definition of a problem usually suggests the policy, but here is an instance where the reverse is true.

The papers in this volume point to an important direction in social policy analysis. This is because they deal with planning, and planning imposes a degree of discipline on the planner; he must ask not only what needs to be done, but what is the optimal way of doing it. This forces the planner (1) to define a goal—some output of education, or health, or what have you, and (2) to find the method that most efficiently achieves this goal—and efficiency is measured by resource cost. There is a trade-off between results and input costs. Politicians have always known this and planners are now learning it.

The approach remains piecemeal. We have not yet really learned how to coordinate social policies, how to plan for the spillover effects of a policy, how to construct a social *program*. We must learn to use care when playing with our new policy toys, our computers, our econometric models, and the kind of amorality that comes from determining what is good for other people. The new technology of social policy can be enormously helpful, but it still provides no magic solutions for ancient problems.

# II

# Health

John R. Moore, Jr., *is assistant professor in the Graduate School of Business and the Department of Community and Preventive Medicine at Stanford University. He attended Purdue University, where he received a B.S. in industrial management, an M.A. in operations research, and the Ph.D. in management science. His past and present research focuses on the design and testing of evaluation techniques for multiple criteria-multiple objective decision problems, and on the application of such analyses to problems in the operation of health services.*

# 2

# Planning An Efficient Regional Health System

JOHN R. MOORE, JR.

## Background

Recognition of the importance of health planning has grown as the national health-care crisis has become more pronounced. Spiraling costs of hospital care, a physician shortage, the clustering of medical resources in suburban and university centers, and the inaccessibility of care to rural communities and the urban poor have fast become facts of American life. Closer study of these problems has suggested that their resolution is more a resource-management problem than one of medical technology.

This paper attempts to define the process of health planning at the local level. For this purpose, the health-planning process is separated into four distinct action phases:

- Stimulus to action
- Assessing the feasibility of intervention
- Plan development
- Plan implementation

In this paper these phases are described and subdivided into a number of steps that should be undertaken by a planning organization.

## Stimulus to Action

An important determinant of the quality as well as the quantity of planning performed by an organization is the process motivating that body to take action on a given problem. For this phase of planning to be done well, an agency must be organized to recognize both obvious and disguised symptoms of health system problems and then to determine the exact nature of the problem for which planning is required.

Since the planning council is frequently the only local organization with comprehensive responsibility for the health system, failure to detect and act upon the symptoms of a developing problem permits the situation to worsen. Where a small problem could have been remedied through a few simple steps by the council, the larger problem will consume large amounts of planning resources and time and, since the problem is now obvious to the public, force the council to work in a politically charged atmosphere.

Even when a planning body is quick to act on a developing problem, it may err by acting on the symptom rather than the root cause. Many local councils have recognized that it is possible to solve the "wrong problem"; for example, in the area of infant illness and mortality, solutions must be sought not only in improved pediatric resources but also in dietary education and better housing.

SYMPTOM RECOGNITION

The symptom-recognition step in health planning is concerned with the way potential or existing health system problems obtain the attention of the planning agency. Although there are several avenues for such recognition, one should predominate. The planning agency should maintain an information system sufficient to allow it to detect problems in its area of responsibility as they are developing. This can be done in two ways.

First, and foremost, the agency should identify those measures of health and health-system performance it wishes to monitor. From these measures it can then be determined which units within the local health system are sources of information necessary to construct the measures. An information-reporting system should then be designed to collect data from operating units and process it for evaluation by the planning council.

Obviously, such a monitoring system will never be possible unless the planning agency has previously established good working relationships with the many organizations active in a local health system. It should be pointed out to every unit from which data is requested that since major health problems do cross organizational lines, early problem detection requires centralized monitoring of the local health system. It is encouraging to note that several Comprehensive Health Planning (CHP) and Regional Medical Program (RMP) groups have succeeded in establishing comprehensive information systems supported by operating units within the health system.

It may not be as obvious, however, that a workable monitoring system should differ from many current ones. These have been criticized as simple aggregations of all available health data, assembled without regard as to how the data will be processed and used. The charge commonly heard is "data for data's sake." To be of value, a monitoring system must collect and process only information on measures that the planning agency wishes to observe and evaluate. Before ever proposing to collect a single item of data, planners must determine the measures they will require for detecting health-system problems. The monitoring process will quickly break down if planners insist upon burying themselves in raw data.

Planners cannot be expected to be prophetic. Although they may go to great effort to construct a comprehensive monitoring system, it is a virtual certainty that some problems will develop unnoticed. Thus, the planning agency should employ a second form of symptom recognition: planners should be receptive and responsive to evidence of problems reported unilaterally from any part of the health system. Again, in this instance, receptivity and response will be enhanced where the planning agency has achieved the cooperation of providers and consumers of health services. Potential problems will be reported quickly when planners have established a reputation of concern for emerging health-system difficulties. The agency will be better able to follow up on reports when a basis for data collection already exists. Requests for additional information will be honored when data sources trust planners to make fair evaluations and to provide opportunity and guidance for corrective action.

Since planning agencies have limited resources, they cannot monitor every potential problem area. A monitoring system should arise from the priorities inherent in the agency's goals. In the case of CHP and RMP, the Department of Health, Education and Welfare has outlined several health problems and target populations to which local monitoring should be sensitive. In addition to these areas, local units must, as a requirement of their organizational grants, develop further statements of objectives, thereby establishing priorities for monitoring.

Local agencies frequently use the organizational period to single out a number of problems for further study. Although this promotes immediate planning activity, it does not constitute comprehensive monitoring. Proceeding as it does, largely without carefully processed health system data, symptom recognition is frequently limited to the scope of experience of the members of the planning agency. Where the organization is broadly representative of the health system, this is not a problem. However, early devotion to specific problem areas still produces an organizational myopia that can discourage sensitivity to newly emerging problems; in short, the agency becomes typecast. In its early days CHP appeared to be concerned exclusively with minority populations since health problems for these persons were often the greatest. This perceived role not only influenced the range of problems referred to local CHP councils but also severely restricted cooperation by many provider groups within the health system.

In summary, a planning agency increases its opportunity to be a positive force for change and improvement of the local health system if symptom recognition is an active rather than passive function. In many local councils planners seem permanently bound to "fire-fighting" duties as a result of waiting for problems to come to them. A surer formula for frustration could probably not be found.

PROBLEM DEFINITION

Problem definition is the process through which recognized symptoms of a health-system problem are investigated and a specific well-defined problem is said to exist. The dimensions of a problem must be stated explicitly and in a manner that facilitates the development of a workable solution. Thus, the concept of a *well-defined* problem is introduced. A health-system problem will be considered well-defined if the following conditions are satisfied:

(1) The organization(s) and specific functions therein having decision responsibility in the area of the problem should be known.

(2) There is agreement as to the measures used to describe and scale the existence and severity of the problem.

(3) The problem is stated in terms of a disparity between health services required and those services the existing system can provide.

The activities of one CHP council provide an example to illustrate the importance of a problem being well defined. As part of its monitoring activities the council noted that, compared with statistics developed nationally and for surrounding urban areas, its region posted an unusually high ratio of accidental-injury deaths to total injuries. In other words, a person suffering an injury locally was more likely to die than if the injury were received elsewhere. The council was rightfully disturbed at such a finding.

In view of this rudimentary information, the problem could have been within the jurisdiction of several organizations. Obvious candidates were the area's hospitals; but which functions within the hospitals? The problem may have been inadequate emergency room procedures for handling shock patients, too few trained traumatic surgeons, or a deficiency in other surgical and recovery care resources within the hospital. Another candidate for organizational responsibility was the ambulance system; accident victims may have had to wait too long for hospital treatment due to equipment shortage, inefficient dispatching, etc.

Since determining organizational responsibility is much like "laying the blame," planners must be careful to use measures of systems performance that properly locate the source of a problem. In this example, the reliability of accident data for other than automobile accidents was so low that it had to be disregarded. Interestingly enough, local performance in national and surrounding area comparisons was slightly poorer when only automobile accident injuries were concerned.

At first, responsibility was attributed to local hospitals. Deaths in the emergency room, during surgery, and after surgery were judged to be very high as a proportion of total injury victims. No particular hospital could be cited as the culprit; all showed uniformly poor performance. Hospital staffs expressed considerable amazement—not to mention hostility —at these findings. It was pointed out, however, that particularly dangerous road conditions in the area might be contributing to more serious injuries, thereby producing faulty inferences from the accident data used. Thus, an improved measure was required—one that reflected hospital performance within limited classes of injury severity.

At this point it should be noted that improved measures of health system performance frequently strain a planning agency's ability to collect data. Since the more common aggregate measures are seldom adequate for detailed problem definition, agencies have to scour the many information services and state and federal agencies for the measures needed. In the example at hand, local planners knew where to look for data and soon learned two things: (1) local hospitals were on or above national averages in saving patients with nearly every kind of injury, and (2) area accidents resulted in more severe injuries than elsewhere in the state. Thus, new organizational units, the state and local highway departments, entered the picture.

The problem had not yet been pinpointed. Although the hospital system had apparently been absolved of responsibility, the ambulance system still stood between the accident scene and hospital treatment. A high DOA (dead on arrival at the hospital) measure caused the council to examine the average time between the accident and the arrival at the scene of an ambulance; performance was very poor. Other measures such as ambulances per 1,000 persons and number of calls received when no vehicle was free focused attention on the patient rescue system. Further deficiencies were then noticed in the level of medical training demonstrated by attendants and in the system of dispatching vehicles owned by cities, hospitals, and several private organizations.

The problem reached a well-defined state when specific deficiencies in the level of attendant training, peak load demand for emergency services and maximum acceptable dispatching delays were identified. It was recommended that road conditions be studied by the appropriate highway divisions.

## Assessing the Feasibility of Intervention

Before detailed planning activity is begun, it should be determined that there is a reasonable chance that results can be implemented and the problem eased or even eliminated. It is important for agencies with limited resources that every dollar and man-hour invested in planning have the greatest possible impact on the health system. Health planning agencies, not unlike corporate planning staffs, frequently suffer the frustration of having carefully developed plans rejected or simply ignored. Thus, a careful choice of problems frequently can be in the best interest of both the planner and the system.

The steps considered appropriate to this planning phase include listing of major alternatives, estimating the resources required by each, and then surveying the available ones to determine if any or all alternatives are feasible. The feasibility test usually takes the form of asking: For each alternative, is it possible that the needed resources can be attracted and appropriately organized in a reasonable period of time?

The three steps described below view the feasibility problem objectively. They force planners to ask if it is physically possible to solve the problem. For the purposes of this study the issue of political feasibility is not treated directly. Nonetheless, it is a part of the planning agency's assessment of the proposed task. The first question that must be faced is whether the agency in question is the proper organization to perform the planning. Since the number of planning groups is legion, it is seldom clear which group has jurisdiction over a given problem. Blurred lines of responsibility underlie much of the confusion and argument surrounding CHP and RMP. In practice, the decision to enter a problem area often is made with a great regard for maintaining cooperation among the members of the health system.

A second and equally important organizational consideration in feasibility assessment concerns the willingness of health system units to implement plans. Although this is an area not considered in this study, it was noted that agency directors could easily identify a number of organizations with which they would find it difficult to work in plan implementation.

LISTING MAJOR ALTERNATIVES

The problem under study has already been explicitly defined in terms of a deficit of health care services available to a target population. In the ambulance service example described above, the problem was stated in terms of a need for vehicles, training and a dispatching system. Alternative programs would involve varying numbers and types of vehicles, different approaches to the training of attendants, and competing systems for dispatching vehicles and crews to an accident scene and then to the appropriate hospital.

At this point in the planning process a preliminary list of alternatives should be proposed. Each program should be stated only in enough detail to permit gross estimates of the resources required to implement such a program. Nonetheless, the feasibility-assessment phase is a good point to begin considering a wide range of alternatives. A small "brainstorming" session may be all that is required to uncover innovative programs that withstand the test of subsequent analysis. One advantage of early identification of major alternatves is that the magnitude of the planning task can then be estimated. It may be that the alternatives involve technology unfamiliar to the planning body or are so complex that the entire effort should be abandoned or outside consultants used. This is obviously an important part of the feasibility assessment.

ESTIMATING RESOURCE REQUIREMENTS

Once alternative programs have been specified, the medical resources required to finance, staff and implement each program must be estimated. Although these initial estimates will necessarily be imprecise, they should reflect more than simply the total cost of each alternative. Estimates should be stated in terms of all resources—levels of manpower, working capital, equipment, buildings, operating systems, and organizations —that a program will require. Cost estimates alone are insufficient for assessing program feasibility. One can easily imagine rural health care programs, calling for only modest funding, that cannot be implemented due to a lack of sufficient medical personnel. Similarly, financial resources may be readily available but only for certain projects. Local tax revenue that would support hospital improvements may not be available for a drug-control program.

SURVEY AVAILABILITY OF RESOURCES

The final step in assessing the feasibility of intervention into a problem is to determine if the area's medical resources are sufficient to satisfy the requirements of one or more of the alternatives thus far proposed. Such a determination requires a survey of the availability of those resources used by alternative programs.

In the case of non-financial resources, planners who are familiar with the local health system can often quickly determine if programs make unrealistic demands. For the ambulance service problem described above, planners would have little difficulty learning earliest delivery dates for vehicles and the size of the labor pool from which attendant trainees could be drawn. A somewhat more political issue would be involved in determining if ambulance owners would accept a centralized dispatch system and if area hospitals would cooperate in the admission of emergency patients.

The survey of financial resources requires a planning staff familiar not only with the local scene but also knowledgeable about the multitude of state, federal, and private foundations' programs for the support of health system projects. Although local tax revenues may be available for the support of a program such as the ambulance project, the survey should be extended in the hope that outside funds can be attracted. This tactic has two benefits: (1) local revenues are "saved" for another project that cannot be funded externally, and (2) the planning agency earns political points it may well need at a later time.

## Plan Development

Once a problem has been defined and intervention by the planning agency judged to be reasonable, full-scale development of a health services plan can commence. For this phase of activity the agency will assemble all the planning resources, such as staff, consultants, advisory committees, project financing, etc., that were thought to be needed during the feasibility-assessment phase.

The planning process described in the following sections is a direct application of what may be termed cost-effectiveness analysis. Once alternative programs have been defined in detail, the effectiveness of each alternative in alleviating the problem is estimated. First the effect of each individual resource employed by an alternative is estimated; then all resources are combined into an operating program. Once the costs of the various alternatives are known it is possible to determine the allocation of resources (alternative program) most appropriate for dealing with the problem. The phrase "most appropriate" suggests that not all planning agencies would implement this process in the same manner. Although several planners may employ the same logical process, their philosophies of planning may be widely different.

A health-services plan has a product objective: the alleviation of some well-defined problem. The act of planning admits to both product and process objectives. Improvement in health and the health system are product objectives; the outline of how planning should be done represents process objectives. But planners also have objectives in planning, often termed philosophies or strategies of planning. Ackoff [1] has identified three major planning strategies: satisficing, optimizing and adaptivizing. A brief description of the three primary planning strategies will facilitate discussion of several steps in the plan-development phase.

When satisficing, the planner selects an alternative that will attain some minimum level of effectiveness but not necessarily exceeding that level. The classical example of satisficing behavior would have a planner accept the first alternative he identifies that (a) he can afford, and (b) achieves the standards of effectiveness he regards as the minimum acceptable. Such a planner would not look further for more effective and/or less costly alternatives; he is not concerned with the trade-off between effectiveness in dealing with a problem and the medical resources consumed by alternative programs. One positive thing can be said for this strategy—it is simple to use, being preferable to no planning at all. However, satisficing does not protect against inefficient allocations of health resources. While it permits identification of the deficiencies of past policies, it does little to insure that future opportunities will be exploited. Such planning is further weakened because it traditionally ignores the possibility of organizational change within the health system and plans for a certain rather than uncertain future. Nonetheless, the logical order of events for a satisficing strategy of planning is essentially described. The primary difference is in the rule the satisficer would use to allocate resources to alternatives.

An optimizing strategy seeks an alternative that in terms of the effectiveness-resource cost trade-ff is in some way the "best." That is, the planner may select the most effective, the least costly, or the most resource-efficient alternative

1. Russel L. Ackoff, *A Concept of Corporate Planning*, Wiley-Interscience: New York, 1970.

program. This is certainly a more complex strategy, but it produces benefits over and above satisficing. By regarding the future as uncertain, the optimizer is more likely to select a flexible program that will not fail if the future is unlike the past. Perhaps its greatest advantage is that the effort reqired to optimize produces a considerably better understanding of the problem area and the trade-offs required by a solution than does satisficing. However, both strategies can employ essentially the same logical processes.

Adaptive or innovative planning is based on the proposition that the value of planning is not the plan that results but the process used to create the plan. Proponents of adaptivizing argue that only a thoroughly rational planning process allows enough understanding of a problem area to permit the creation of an organization and management system that minimizes the need for further retrospective planning. Adaptive planning combines the optimizer's willingness to plan for an uncertain future with a desire to create organizational flexibility. Thus, such a planning strategy does not take the structure of the health system for granted; instead, it builds motivation or incentives for change into a plan. The process of plan development recommended here is general enough to serve even this most ambitious planning strategy.

LISTING ALTERNATIVE RESOURCE CONFIGURATIONS

The first step in full-scale plan development requires that all alternative programs (*i.e.*, configurations of medical resources) that are to be evaluated be explicitly defined. This extends the listing process of the previous phase while differing in two respects. First, alternative programs must be specified in greater detail than before. The specific resources required (though not their quantity) and a plan for organizing those resources should be made explicit. Second, in the active planning phase, extensive search for new alternatives is clearly justified, particularly if an optimizing or adaptive planning strategy is being followed. Ideas previously regarded as poorly formulated must be investigated and either rejected as not feasible or fully specified as alternatives.

Emphasis in the definition of programs should be on the specific health resources to be employed, their organization into definable health services and the target populations to be served. For the ambulance service example, one alternative program might be defined as consisting of the following components:

- Three separate ambulance services to meet the varied needs of the community for patient transport.

  Two-man accident service units staffed with former armed services medics or those similarly trained in the treatment of fractures, laceration, concussion, shock, blood loss, rescue, and removal of the injured.

  Two-man medical service units staffed by one intern and one nurse for calls related to cardiac attack, seizure, stroke, pregnancy, and other non-accident needs.

  Two-man transport service units staffed by medical aides for non-emergency transport of patients to hospitals or other care facilities.

- Accident service vehicles owned and operated by municipal governments and equipped for patient rescue, removal, and on-site treatment.

- Medical-service vehicles owned and operated by the area-wide association of hospitals and equipped for emergency medical treatment.

- Transport service vehicles owned and operated privately by ambulance services and morticians with state licensing of equipment and crew standards.

- Physicians, shock therapists, and nurses organized into three ambulance-crew training programs administered by a single local hospital.

- Central and remote radio equipment for dispatching vehicles and crews in response to a call for service.

- Computer devices and necessary system support to help the dispatcher select an appropriate service unit, route it to the call, and designate a receiving hospital.

- Radio dispatch personnel.

The level of detail illustrated here is necessary. Without it, for instance, it would not be possible to examine differences in cost and effectiveness among different patterns of crew composition or vehicle ownership.

## DETERMINE RESOURCE PRODUCTIVITY

The previous step will produce a list of alternative resources for which estimates of productivity or "service capacity" must be obtained. In other words, for a unit of a specified resource, the planning agency must determine how much service that resource can provide. For example, with central dispatching services in operation a transport service unit may be capable of completing 30 calls per 24-hour day whereas the accident service unit could complete 16 calls.

The determination of resource productivity requires definition of the units of measure that will eventually form the basis for all future analysis and decision-making as well as evaluation of the resulting operating program. The ambulance problem, for instance, is not strictly one of insuring that a minimum number of calls can be answered in a given day. A new program must demonstrate that the appropriate medical equipment and talent can be delivered to the scene of an emergency in a reasonable amount of time. Resource productivity depends on the volume of calls and the number of units in service as well as those units' reaction time. Productivity estimates can be determined by a simple simulation model that will produce for a likely pattern of calls a response time (call to arrival) *as a function* of the number of units of each type that are placed in service. Clearly, a time-per-unit figure would be meaningless since, over a given range, response time would decrease as the number of available units increased.

Finally, it should be anticipated that the productivity of a given resource will depend upon its type. An ambulance can make more calls if it is in simple transport service rather than emergency or accident use. The response time of all system units may decrease if the dispatching system is replaced by a decentralized calling system.

ASSESS THE EFFECTIVENESS OF ALTERNATIVES

Once estimates of resource productivity have been made, it is then necessary to develop another measure that describes the effectiveness (utility or value to the community) of providing services over the ranges considered by the alternative programs. This new measure is needed since alternative programs may provide different services to different target populations and are, therefore, not immediately comparable. For comparability to exist it is usually necessary to develop a common measure into which the benefits of alternative programs can be translated. Only in the most narrowly defined problem situations is it imaginable that programs will be comparable without this translation.

In the ambulance example, the program alternative that was defined in a previous step deals with three target populations: victims of accidents, other medical emergencies, and patients requiring simple transport. It would be difficult to compare this program with another that was directed only at accident victims. Certainly the time required to respond to a call would not be an adequate basis for comparison since one program may be slower to respond but serve many more individuals. In fact, time to respond is inconsequential for patients requiring only simple transportation.

One possible measure of effectiveness that could be used to compare alternatives such as these is a fairly simple point system to score programs. One scoring system would award points based on the average response time required to deliver the appropriate medical aid to accident victims or other emergency cases. Point values would decrease with increasing response time, as illustrated below:

| Response Time | Point Value |
|---|---|
| 0- 5 minutes | 10 |
| 5-10 minutes | 9 |
| 10-15 minutes | 8 |
| 15-20 minutes | 6 |
| 20-25 minutes | 4 |
| 25-30 minutes | 2 |
| Over 30 minutes | 1 |

Patients provided with transport service would receive a score of, say, three points. A total program-effectiveness score would then be determined by multiplying the number of persons receiving each service by the point score for that service. As a result, programs would be made comparable on a basis that reflected quality of service as well as the volume of services provided.

Obviously, more elaborate effectiveness measures can be devised for the ambulance program. Planners should take care, however, that the measures they employ are not unwieldy or difficult to interpret. The temptation to develop a formal masterpiece as a measurement scheme is often irresistible, particularly for outside consultants.

ESTIMATION OF PROGRAM COSTS

Before a program alternative can be selected the resource costs of each program must be estimated. A cost function must be developed that accurately describes the expense of establishing and operating alternative programs at various feasible levels of resource utilization. The functional representation is necessary since in the planning step where alternatives were defined only the resource configurations were specified, not the scale of those configurations. Thus, in the ambulance program the existence of three two-man service units was proposed but the specific number of trained crews and vehicles was left open. Had this not been done, there would have been an absurdly large number of different alternatives. A program with ten accident crews and eight emergency teams would have been different from a program using nine of each crew. As a result, only major distinct alternatives are recognized.

However, another and more important reason underlies the way in which alternatives are defined. As the scale of a configuration changes, one would expect effectiveness to vary. Adding more ambulances should improve the program effectiveness measure. But an increase in effectiveness comes only with increased resource cost. The value of this definition of the planning process is that it places emphasis on the trade-off between cost and effectiveness. This discourages satisficing, simplifies the determination of a proper level at which a program should operate, and encourages efficient use of medical resources.

PROGRAM SELECTION

The necessary groundwork has now been done, and the planning agency can select the program it wishes to implement. The information assembled consists of costs of various levels of program activity, measures of effectiveness of alternative resources, and the availability of medical resources required by the programs under consideration. The selection problem is a classical resource allocation problem. Financial and other medical resources are expended to buy effectiveness in solving a well-defined health-system problem.

The planner must now select a decision rule that will guide the allocation process. A satisficing strategy merely requires that resources be added to the various alternatives until one program produces an acceptable effectiveness rating. However, since the satisficer has gone to the effort of assembling the information available at this stage, he can easily afford to become an optimizer.

While the optimizing strategy of planning presents a variety of rules for selecting programs, it also affords the planner an opportunity to learn a great deal more about the decision he must make. Two rules are used most commonly in program selection. The first is but a simple modification of the satisficing strategy. This rule selects that program achieving a minimum acceptable level of effectiveness at the lowest possible cost, subject to constraints on the availability of non-financial medical resources. The second rule is complementary; it maximizes program effectiveness subject to limitations on budgets and other resources. Both of these rules suggest linear- or integer-programming formulations to determine levels of resource commitment, although such elaborate technology is not required when the number of alternatives is small.

The planner need not be committed to either rule, however. A useful analytical device, illustrated in Figure 2.1, is to

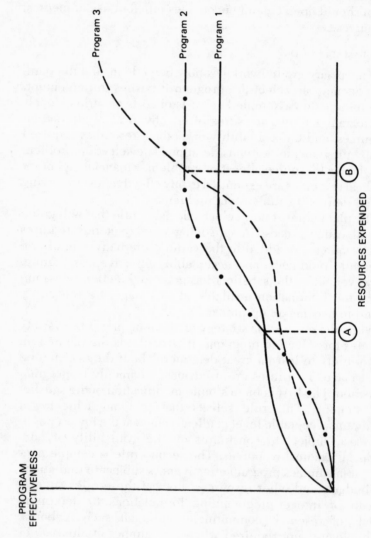

FIGURE 2.1 Comparison for Program Selection

compute the effectiveness resulting from each program over a range of resource levels. This produces a graphic means of comparing programs. One interpretation of Figure 2.1 is that for any level of resource expenditure up to amount A, Program 1 is clearly preferred. However, above the budget level Program 2 dominates all other alternatives until resource commitment reaches an amount B. At this point Program 3, which never looked very promising before, becomes the preferred alternative. Such an approach to this decision problem allows the planning agency to construct, when needed, forceful arguments for additional resources by showing the incremental benefits that can be earned.

## Plan Implementation

Health-planning agencies are often accused of working in a vacuum; that is, they observe a problem, develop plans for resolving it, and then abandon both problem and plans for activities in another area. The history of federally sponsored health planning suggests that if plans are ever to become reality, the planning organization must direct implementation efforts. Far from being a separate and avoidable duty, implementation is a central part of the planning process, requiring decision-making and the design of organizations for the long-term operation of new programs. In a sense, planning for a given problem is never finished. Since the problem environment is constantly changing, it is important that a system be provided for maintaining the plan, thereby eliminating the need for further retrospective planning. This is synonymous with implementation.

While it is important that an agency actively plan for implementation, it is almost universally agreed that planners should not become deeply involved in the operation of health-services programs. RMP is a notable exception in this regard. Several area offices have developed programs which they have proceeded to implement and operate. CHP has shown a marked preference—in part due to tight budgeting—for delegating operating responsibility to new or existing organizations.

It is not surprising that implementation is a highly political activity, more so than even problem definition. The first step in this phase requires that agreement as to the suitability of the plan be reached by other organizations concerned with the health system. Only when this is done can planners proceed to give long-term responsibility for the program being installed to an existing body or a new operating group. Finally, resources can be attracted and committed to the project and the progress in implementation monitored.

COORDINATE COOPERATING INSTITUTIONS

Once a plan has been selected the planning agency should immediately identify those groups and institutions whose cooperation is vital to the success of the plan and then move to insure that cooperation will be forthcoming. Perhaps the most successful strategy for gaining cooperation is to involve these organizations in early phases of the planning process when problems are identified, alternatives explored, and final plans selected. Thus, the CHP model of establishing cooperative arrangements among groups within the health system should result in a good basis for plan implementation.

It is important that all groups that may contribute to or be affected by the proposed program reach some consensus about the appropriateness of the plan. If objections are particularly strong, a small amount of time invested in further plan-development activities should prevent substantial losses from occurring when an embattled program fails. In the case of the ambulance program described above, a great amount of trust had to be established among planners, municipalities, and independent ambulance operators before the operators would agree to a central dispatching system. Since the dispatch service was to become a public office, it appeared to the private service owners that they would be the last to be called when transport service was requested. When the necessary accommodations were made, objections ceased.

DESIGNATE AN OPERATING GROUP

The configuration of resources in the program selected will, in part, suggest the organization responsible for implementing and operating the program. This may be an existing institution, in which case the planning agency must offer assistance in reorganizing around a new function as well as consulting on issues of timing, inter-agency cooperation, and progress monitoring. In the ambulance example, one local hospital becomes responsible for conducting a training program for attendants. The planning agency should advise that hospital on the annual graduation rate needed to sustain the program, the level of training prospective students can be expected to have, and means of attracting trainees. Given the conditions of the funding for this program, the planning agency will also have to negotiate the amount, if any, that the hospital will be reimbursed for offering the training program.

Where new organizations are required to operate a program, the planning agency must take an active role along with cooperating institutions in the definition of the structure and the staffing of these new groups. We know of instances wherein a program failed because a newly created operating unit did not integrate well with the rest of the units in the program. This is often as much due to poor organization or staffing as to political reasons. Again returning to the ambulance problem, the way in which the new dispatching service was organized and functioned was very important to the success of the entire program. Private ambulance service owners did not trust the dispatching system, if operated as a public department similar to a county public health office, to act in their interests. The prevalent suspicion was that publicly owned vehicles would, when idle, be used for transport duties rather than being strictly limited to emergency calls. In this way private operators would receive very little business. Therefore, it fell to the planners to define the operations of the dispatching service so that private operators would work within the program, thereby benefiting all of the proposed services.

ATTRACT RESOURCES

The planning agency has already identified possible sources
of program funding during the feasibility-assessment phase.
It should now join with the newly formed operating groups
to attract and commit the needed funding as well as other
medical resources. In the funding area, many planning bodies
are extremely knowledgeable and practiced at obtaining
grants, contracts, and other forms of program support.
Community-based planners have spent years developing relationships among local government, civic, and business groups.
These relationships often prove useful when program funding
is required. Further, when planning has been done analyti-
cally, as recommended here, the planning agency can usually
be an effective sales representative to skeptical sponsors.

Some planning agencies exhibit greater effectiveness than
others in attracting program funding. Hospital-planning
associations develop new systems for one or more hospitals
that require no outside funding. Where a number of facilities
are involved in a plan, a consortium is easily formed to determine each member's share of the costs and administrative
duties. Several RMP groups sponsor programs directly from
their budgets or through project grants. Charitable organizations and CHP councils frequently look to community sources
of project funding, at times with little success.

MONITOR IMPLEMENTATION AND OPERATION

The planning agency does not physically install the new program; this duty falls to the operating group. However, the
planners must keep a watchful eye on the implementation
process and be ready to question and advise the operating
group when necessary. As in the symptom-recognition step,
problems are most easily resolved when they are detected
early. Schedule slippage and budget overrun are frequently
signs of faulty estimation. Such signals must be studied quickly
to determine if implementation should proceed or if new programs should be considered.

The planning agency proposed the new program in response to a problem that had been detected and identified. The agency should monitor the program, when it passes into the operational stage, to determine if it functions as expected and if it is effective in alleviating the problem in question. In situations where problem monitoring is through stable measures of health status, little change will be noticed. However, intermediate measures such as those used in estimating resource productivity and program effectiveness may be used to check the program's operation. Another monitoring device often used is a requirement that the operating group submit periodic evaluations of the program.

The process outlined here is one possible way in which area-wide health-services planning might be conducted. It embodies an orderly, analytic approach to the solution of complex health-system problems that should enable planning agencies to realize the greatest benefit from their limited resources. Planners employing less systematic processes frequently spend inordinate amounts of time in needless or repetitive activities. The procedure recommended here focuses upon those actions essential to the development of a viable health-services plan.

Judith R. Lave *is an assistant professor of economics and public affairs at the Graduate School of Industrial Administration and School of Urban and Public Affairs, Carnegie-Mellon University. Queen's University granted her an M.A. and Ph.D. She has worked for National Blue Cross and received grants from Blue Cross of Western Pennsylvania and the Health Information Foundation. With her husband, she is principal investigator of a project to examine hospital cost and production functions, sponsored by the National Center for Health Services Research and Development, and is also conducting research on the implementation of a management information system at Presbyterian-University Hospital and on the delivery of ambulatory care. Dr. Lave has published widely on the economics of health, is on the editorial board of* Health Services Review, *and is a consultant to a number of government agencies and private companies.*

Lester B. Lave *is professor of economics and head of the department of economics at the Graduate School of Industrial Administration, Carnegie-Mellon University. His B.A. is from Reed College and his Ph.D. is from Harvard University. Dr. Lave's work is focused on quantifying information necessary for making good public decisions. He has had grants from a variety of sponsors such as the National Institute of Mental Health, the National Safety Council, Resources for the Future, Inc., the Office of the Secretary, HEW, and the National Center for Health Services Research and Development. Dr. Lave is author of numerous publications ranging from the value of better weather information to the raisin industry to a book on technological change. He is currently a member of the National Research Council.*

Thomas E. Morton *is associate professor of industrial administration at Carnegie-Mellon University. He holds the B.A. in mathematics from California Institute of Technology, an M.S. in mathematics from the University of Chicago, and both the M.B.A. and Ph.D. from Chicago's Graduate School of Business. He has published several articles in the area of operations research.*

# 3

# Sources and Uses of Paramedical Personnel

JUDITH R. LAVE, LESTER B. LAVE,
AND THOMAS E. MORTON

## Introduction

The shortage, maldistribution, and inefficient use of physicians
—particularly primary physicians—has received much attention recently. Suggested solutions focus on either increasing
the number of physicians or the efficiency with which primary
medical care services are produced. The number of physicians
can be increased by enlarging the class size in medical schools,
establishing more medical schools, or shortening the training
period. These relatively conservative solutions involve
expanding the current system without making basic changes.
Solutions which require basic changes in the way medical
care is delivered include increasing the physician's efficiency
through the use of assistants, analyzing and rearranging physician tasks, and changing the physician's role as the primary
person interacting with the patient.

This report concentrates on the second group of solutions,
specifically on increasing physician efficiency through the
development of the "paramedic"—a health care worker who
performs primary-care tasks formerly reserved for the physi-

Previously published in a condensed form as "The Physician's Assistant:
Exploration of the Concept" in *Hospitals, J. Am. Hosp. Assc.*, 45:42-51.

cian. Only health workers interacting with patients are considered, including nurses in expanded roles such as nurse-
midwives and Pediatric Nurse Practitioners (PNP's). (Controversy surrounds the name for such a worker. We will use
the generic *paramedic*, but in citing specific studies or programs we will use the name assumed therein.) Task analysis
has shown that many of a physician's duties can successfully
be delegated to a person with less training without significantly
increasing either the risk of an unsatisfactory outcome or
patient discomfort. The paramedic can release appreciable
physician time, in some tasks almost on a one-to-one basis.
Paramedics can also be used to: (*a*) increase the profitability
of a practice, (*b*) reduce strain on other health workers, and
(*c*) perform some important aspects of medical care which formerly were neglected.

The issues surrounding the use of paramedic personnel are
complex and fundamental to the way medical care is to be
delivered. There is disagreement about the name and definition of paramedic, the tasks they should perform, the amount
of prior training and experience they require, the additional
training they will need, their acceptance by both patients and
other deliverers of health care, and their relationship to the
physician. This report will explore each of these issues. For
each issue, we raise the central problem and then discuss
the literature which is relevant to it. While we try to clarify
the implications of the various issues, this report will not
attempt to reconcile all the controversies. It is important to
note that published papers are basically supportive of the
paramedic.

## Background

PHYSICIAN SHORTAGE

Although researchers do not agree on the existence of a physician shortage, they generally concur that there is a maldistribution of physicians among the specialties and by location. There
is a crisis in the availability of practitioners providing family
care for many Americans. The introduction of the paramedic

into American medicine is primarily a response to the perceived shortage of physicians and the lack of adequate family health care.

Knowles [39] documents both the physician shortage and the maldistribution of physicians, and presents a good bibliography on the health manpower shortage issue. The Bane Report [8] and the first two volumes of the 1967 Report of the National Advisory Commission of Health Manpower [55] also document the shortage. According to Fein [22, Ch. 1] the shortage problem depends partly on definition but at current prices the demand for physician services exceeds the supply. He projects that from 1965 to 1975 demand will increase from 22 to 26 percent while the supply will increase only 13 percent, excluding foreign physicians who immigrate, or 19 percent including immigrants [27, Ch. 5].

If the market is the criterion, Hansen [30] disagrees with Fein, maintaining that no shortage exists and that physicians do not earn a high rate of return on their investment in medical education. Presumably, Hansen would argue that unless lower quality applicants were taken, the training period shortened, or other factors changed, increasing the supply of physicians would be difficult.

Ginzberg [27, 28] has argued most consistently against the existence of a physician shortage. He believes that the problem is "excess demand," not "deficient supply." Over-doctoring takes the form of unnecessary visits, unnecessary surgery, the fashionable annual physical, and certain types of well care. Much of this excess demand stems from physicians' advising their patients to seek additional services.

While arguing that there is no overall shortage, Ginzberg does indicate that physicians are badly distributed. However, his solution to the maldistribution problem is not to increase the supply of physicians, which would result only in more over-doctoring and higher health costs, but to increase the income of the poor, control drug abuse, and generally improve the basic health level of all people. He feels that medical services in the ghetto can be improved by upgrading the public health nurse and giving scholarships to medical students, conditional upon serving an internship in the ghetto. Whatever the general disagreements, it is evident that the delivery of medical care would be improved by a better distribution of physicians across geographic areas and specializations.

INTRODUCTION OF THE PARAMEDIC

The development of paramedics is a partial solution to the perceived shortage of physicians and to the existing maldistribution of physicians, both by location and specialty. Where it is impossible to provide easy access to physicians, such as in rural areas, a paramedic can be trained to provide a high level of service, referring more difficult cases to his supervising physician. Paramedics can be trained to assume many primary care tasks with a resulting improvement in some aspects of the quality of care, improvement in patient satisfaction, and more time for the specialist to perform the complex tasks that he was specifically trained to accomplish.

The paramedic concept is not new. In most European countries, including many with much lower infant mortality rates than our own, deliveries are usually performed by nurse-midwives, with an obstetrician on call for difficult deliveries [40]. The Soviet Union has a health service personnel category called a "feldsher," as well as different classes of physicians [24]. Roughly an equal number of physicians and feldshers are graduated each year with two and one-half years of medical school for the feldsher and six for a physician. Feldshers act as physician assistants in urban areas, while in rural areas they are quite autonomous, treating most routine cases without referral [58, 59].

In the United States nurses and allied health personnel are already assuming many tasks once considered the sole province of the physician. As the skills and training of the physician (and his assistants) have improved, part of the physician's work (such as giving intravenous injections and taking blood) has been delegated. The public health nurse, medical corpsmen, and organizations such as the Frontier Nursing Service of Leslie County, Kentucky, are assuming the paramedic role when necessary. Hence, while the paramedic concept is not new, the recent formalization of various training programs and the support given by organized medicine is new.

## Programs and Demonstration Projects

Many programs to train nurses, corpsmen, and others as paramedics have been established. Kadish and Long [36] have reviewed these programs briefly, and the Professional Activities Branch of the Department of Health, Education and Welfare [52] has released a partial listing of such programs, including their stage of development, curriculum, certificate award, and program director. Ledney [40] lists the midwife training programs. Position statements containing guidelines for the definition and education of various kinds of paramedics have been issued by some of the national professional organizations including: the American Medical Association [1], the Board of Medicine of the National Academy of Sciences [10], the Association of American Medical Colleges [53], the American Academy of Pediatrics [4] and the American Society of Internal Medicine [59]. Collins and Bonnyman [12] compare the types of programs offered with the recommendations of the various professional organizations.

The training period of most existing paramedic programs is either about four months or two to three years. The short-term programs take highly trained, experienced students and give them a new orientation, some didactic training, and new clinical skills. The short training period means that the corpsmen entering Medex or the nurse entering a nurse-practitioner program must be initially highly qualified. The longer programs take applicants with much less training (two years of college "pre-med" or some practical experience as a corpsman or LPN) and give them roughly one year of didactics, one year of clinical training, and one year of internship.

## Potential Role of Paramedics

MANPOWER FOR TRAINING

Little work has been done on the cost of paramedic training. (Two PNP programs were estimated to cost about $1,000 for four months' training.) The physician's assistant (PA) program at Duke University is estimated to require about the same resources per year to train a PA as to train a medical student [34, p. 51]. Since it takes from five to seven years to train most physicians, one less physician must be trained for every three PA's trained.

This latter comparison makes it evident that, without an expansion of medical schools and faculties, it will be difficult to increase significantly the number of two-year programs. Even the PNP programs consume educational resources and so a major expansion of these programs would require some adjustment in medical schools and teaching hospitals. Over the next five to ten years, short-term programs (particularly those taking registered nurses) can be the only important source of paramedics.

Discharged corpsmen are not an important source of candidates for these short programs. Some confusion exists about the potential supply of highly skilled medical corpsmen who are qualified for short programs such as Medex. Approximately 32,000 men with some medical care experience leave the service annually. (About 10,000 have enough primary-care experience to make them potential candidates for two-year training programs, such as that at Duke University [34, p. 49]. A much smaller number have enough training and independent duty experience to qualify for Medex.)

If one considers numbers alone, the registered nurse seems the only potential source for large numbers of paramedic personnel in the short run. The AMA has recently taken a strong position on expanding the nurse's duties [3, 48]. Dr. Ernest B. Howard, Executive Vice President, has stated, "it is the conviction of many in the AMA that with only modest additional training, 100,000 nurses could become associated with physicians in such a way as to expand markedly the physician's ability to serve his patients" [35]. The AMA statement also indicates that, since nurse-practice acts are rather vague on the functions of an RN, licensure problems would be minimal.

The main objections to using nurses as paramedics have come from organized nursing associations such as the ANA which maintain: (1) the nursing shortage would be intensified, (2) legal difficulties might arise, and (3) the position of nursing as an independent profession would be endangered [2]. The ANA estimates that in 1968 there were 613,188 active nurses (of whom 47,628 worked in private offices) and 285,791 inactive nurses [5a, pp. 11 - 16]. The upgrading of 100,000 nurses to paramedic status would seem to be too major a loss for nursing to absorb. However, Yankauer, a strong proponent of using nurses as paramedics, argues that many nurses have retired because of low pay and often tedious duties and that many would return if both pay and job interest were upgraded. (See for example [7, p. 878] and [65, pp. 548 - 550].) However, little research has been done to determine how much higher salaries and changes in duties would effect a return to nursing careers. Additional arguments for using the nurse as the basic source for paramedics include: (1) there will never be a shortage of women entering the nursing profession and (2) the nurse is already an accepted member of the medical team and could move into the new role with comparatively little difficulty.

The proponents of longer programs which do not require applicants to have had nurse training argue: (1) nurses do not make good paramedics because nursing is hierarchical and is becoming more rigid and because women are not interested in professional careers; (2) longer training programs can be more innovative (by formulating an entire curriculum instead of a four-month supplement); and (3) the potential supply of paramedics will be larger if the program is two years instead of nurse training plus four months. Many of these arguments seem to stem from personal experience, rather than any systematic study. (See for example [39, p. 49] and [63].)

Registered nurses, we would argue, are the only important source of paramedics over the next five to ten years. As shown in the section below on acceptance of paramedics, careful evaluation of nurse paramedics suggests that they can provide a high level of medical care and be accepted by both physicians and patients. It is evident that nurse-paramedic programs must receive major attention now, but the longer programs should not be allowed to lapse, since they hold the potential for a different type of paramedic drawn from a different manpower pool.

## POTENTIAL FUNCTIONS OF PARAMEDICS

Depending on the applicant's qualifications and the length of the training program, a paramedic can be trained to do virtually any tasks ranging from taking temperatures to performing thoracic surgery. The former could be done by almost anyone after five minutes training, while the latter would require a very special applicant and nine years of training beyond college (and be indistinguishable from a medical student). To specify the best training program and set of tasks, one must first know the capabilities of the student and the tasks the physician is willing to delegate. Since paramedics are a new personnel category and involve the medical and economic self-interests of the physician, little agreement exists on the exact tasks the paramedic should perform. Much more experience with paramedics of various levels is needed to determine their best role. One beginning step would be to: (1) rank the individual tasks done by each type of physician according to increasing difficulty in terms of judgment and technique, and (2) assess how much judgment, physical skill, and independence can reasonably be expected from a nurse with four months of additional training or an ex-corpsman with two years of supplemental training.

The potential functions of paramedics are also partially dependent on which primary-care tasks physicians are willing to delegate. Yankauer *et al*. [65, 66] determined the percentage of physicians willing to delegate specific tasks (Table I). Interestingly, the academic pediatricians believed more tasks could be delegated than did practicing physicians [66, p. 739]. In a survey of practicing Wisconsin physicians by Coye and Hansen, most physicians approved of an assistant's taking a medical history but were opposed to allowing the paramedic to give routine anesthetics, perform ordinary deliveries, or do portions of physical examinations [13]. Yet many medical educators regard taking a medical history as a task that demands the doctor's judgment; the latter tasks are more routine, although each has more potential danger and requires more technical training.

With regard to the paramedic's level of independence and authority, there is much more disagreement. The physician's assistants at Duke University and the pediatric nurse-practitioners at the Massachusetts General program, for example, are trained to assume "dependent" roles as physician's assistants who carry out assigned tasks. The pediatric nurse-practitioners at the University of Colorado and the child health associates at the University of Colorado are trained to be more independent (but not independent in the manner of a chiropractor).

TABLE 3.1   *Current Office Patient Care Tasks*

|  | *Percent Pediatricians Delegating Task* | *Percent Pediatricians Favoring Delegation** |
|---|---|---|
| Information/Children | 29 | 92 |
| Information/Immunization | 43 | 90 |
| Interpret Instruction | 31 | 85 |
| Telephone/Child-care | 47 | 78 |
| Family Social History | 42 | 75 |
| | | |
| Interval History/Well Child | 18 | 65 |
| Past Medical History | 32 | 63 |
| Advice/Feeding—Development | 22 | 62 |
| Telephone/Minor Medical Advice | 53 | 59 |
| Advice/Minor Medical | 52 | 52 |
| | | |
| Interval/History Sick Child | 15 | 45 |
| Advice/School Child | 9 | 40 |
| Present Illness History | 25 | 39 |
| Exam/Well Child | 9 | 25 |
| Exam/Sick Child | 12 | 19 |

*These are approximate figures derived from a bar chart.
SOURCE: Yankauer, *et al.* [65, p. 540].

Physicians oppose the autonomous paramedic for a host of reasons which are a mixture of professional concern and economic self-interest. (Coye and Hansen find that no anesthesiologists believe assistants should give anesthetics, and only two percent of obstetricians believe assistants should deliver babies. Yet 8 percent of physicians as a group would delegate anesthesia, and 12 percent would delegate an uncomplicated delivery [13, p. 531].) It is certainly no accident that most "autonomous" paramedics find service in rural and ghetto areas.

The willingness of physicians to delegate tasks to a paramedic is surely a complicated function of legal liability, peer-group pressure, patient attitudes, expectation of the quality of care delivered by the paramedic, and the number of hours in the physician's work week. While some office nurses and public health nurses have assumed many primary-care tasks, few physicians have hired and trained nurses for these tasks. Their failure to do so probably reflects fear of malpractice suits, the fact that physicians have little training in delegation, fear that the paramedic won't give high-quality care, and other such factors, rather than an unwillingness to delegate taking histories, giving shots, and checking on a patient's progress. (This is partly borne out by the report that physicians who have worked with paramedics in demonstration projects have grown more willing to delegate tasks, even if they were initially hostile to the paramedic concept. See for example [23, p. 1099].)

It is an important economic insight that various medical inputs—the nurse, the aide, the physician—can all be combined in different ways to restore health. For example, a routine physical examination can be performed solely by a physician, by a nurse-physician combination where the history, weight, height, and temperature are taken by the nurse, or by a physician-nurse-technician combination where the assistants perform a number of tests and the role of the physician is restricted to the interpretation of the tests. These different ways of delivering the same service can be designed to provide medical care of a similar quality but with vastly different implications for cost and utilization of scarce resources such as physician time. We believe that the current interest in paramedics should be justified by their potential to produce medical care in many different ways, potentially saving much physician time and increasing the efficiency of producing medical services.

Medicine is unique among manufacturing and service industries in the United States in that there is no gradation of skill and training levels. The physician has at least 21 years of education, and generally 24 or more. In an office setting, the next highest educational level is usually his secretary with perhaps 12 years of training and occasionally a nurse with 15 years of education. Even in an institutional setting, the next highest level of training is 15 or 16 years. There is no reason to believe that all of the 24 years of training are necessary for most of the tasks performed by the physician.

Improvements in medical-care delivery have been impeded in that many innovations are slow to be adopted since physicians do not have the time to search for them or to train new personnel to apply them. Increasing the number of paramedics and other assistants would result in people with more diverse kinds and levels of training; it would permit innovations to be adopted more rapidly and rationally. These paramedics could also do a more thorough job in counseling, health education, and various preventive health measures.

QUALITY OF CARE

In discussing how the introduction of the paramedic will affect the quality of care, one might distinguish three dimensions of quality: the social and psychological aspects of care; the medical efficacy of the care; and quality of care as perceived by the patient.

Medical care involves a great deal more than surgical repair or the diagnosis and treatment of an acute condition. Most medical care is palliative and affects neither the severity nor the duration of the disease. Patients must be informed about the nature of their illness and helped to adjust to chronic illness and recover from surgery. Paramedics who have special training or additional time for the patient can perform many of these tasks better than a physician. Delegation of these tasks can improve the quality of care, increase patient satisfaction, and free the physician to perform more complicated tasks.

In evaluating medical efficacy, one must look at care under real, rather than ideal, conditions. While a board-certified pediatrician doing a workup on a well baby in a teaching hospital can do a much better and more thorough job than a paramedic, the relevant comparison is whether the pediatrician in his office does a better and more thorough job.

Virtually all reported experience with paramedics is with specially trained nurses. Thus, it is difficult to distinguish good paramedic care from good nursing care. It is possible that what the patients really need is good nursing care, a service neither physicians nor paramedics (except those with good nursing backgrounds) are prepared to deliver. This objection cannot be answered without more evaluations of the non-nurse paramedic.

The evidence suggests that quality of care need not decline if paramedics are introduced. The paramedic is trained to be cautious. Lewis *et al.* [43] compared the outcome of care for chronic patients provided at a *nurse* clinic with that provided at a regular medical clinic. Most chronic patients treated by the nurse-clinicians reported a significant reduction of discomfort and many were able to return to work or find employment. Some patients in the control clinics left jobs and most experienced no change in discomfort, as expressed by frequency of complaints. The authors argue that differences in outcome were "related not to the patients selected for the study or to the abilities of the practitioners caring for them but to the different processes of care emphasized by physicians and nurses" [43, p. 648].

Duncan *et al.* [18] reviewed 182 charts of children seen first by a pediatric nurse and subsequently by a pediatrician. The pediatrician observed a total of 278 conditions, of which 239 were in total agreement with the findings of the PNP. Of the 39 differences in assessment, 37 were judged not significant. (Usually the PNP assessed more conservatively. For example, she felt tympanic membranes sufficiently infected for referral, an incorrect judgment according to the physician.) In one case of significant difference the PNP believed an erythema of the throat to be the primary site of the child's illness and thought the child ill enough to be seen immediately by the physician; the physician diagnosed pneumonia. In the other case, the PNP evaluated a boy with a fever and erythema of the throat. She did not feel the child was ill enough for immediate referral and suggested he return the next day. During the night the child developed acute symptoms and was seen by a physician, who incorrectly diagnosed meningitis. (The researchers expressed doubt that the findings of two physicians would be as close.)

These results indicate that the quality of medical care need not be impaired when a paramedic assumes the primary-care role. Each paramedic is trained to refer the patient to a physician when there is any doubt. Indeed, as evidenced below in the section on patient acceptance, paramedics may actually provide better-quality care than physicians since: (1) they can spend more time with the patient and so can more fully explore possible medical difficulties and (2) they often provide a more relaxed atmosphere in which the patient feels free to ask additional questions about health matters.

The paramedic might engender a slightly increased probability of an incorrect assessment or incorrect suggested treatment when compared to a physician. The risk, however, is small enough that no one, for example, would seriously advocate forbidding registered nurses to give shots or perform other routine tasks. A board-certified pediatrician who spent the same amount of time with each child as the paramedic will probably make fewer assessment and treatment errors. However, the difference in quality of care is likely to be small and, in practice, the pediatrician spends much less time with the child. The question then becomes whether we are willing to tolerate the slight potential increase in risk with using a paramedic for the potential gain in health-care delivery.

Thus, the answer to the question of "what tasks might be delegated to the paramedic?" is all those tasks that the paramedic can perform with essentially the same risk level as a physician.

## Acceptance of Paramedics

There is now general acceptance of paramedics in a dependent role in organized medicine. The AMA [1] and the American Academy of Pediatrics [4] have endorsed such roles strongly. There is much more hesitation in accepting the independent paramedic.

A major conflict centers around nurse-midwives. The American College of Obstetricians and Gynecologists has refused to take a stand. There is ample evidence that a well-trained nurse-midwife can handle most deliveries [40, 37], yet many states bar them.

Physicians who have worked with paramedics are reported to be favorable in their attitudes. Even physicians who were initially suspicious accepted the paramedics [43]. However, Resnick [56] reports that some physicians expressed hostility to the nurse-practitioner, claiming that she was practicing medicine illegally. Other physicians are reported to oppose the concept [14, 64]. Much of the controversy centers around the quality-of-care issue. Since some physicians assume that the paramedics provide medicine of low quality, they oppose the introduction of a second-class medical system. Rather than continue to review these fears, we point out the evidence on the quality of care in the previous section and the evidence on patient acceptance in the following section. We would also point out that general acceptance will depend partly on one's philosophy towards medical care. Stead has succinctly put the point this way [63, p. 207]:

> We do have a difference in point of view between those people who believe the past can be recreated and shored up by tinkering with it here or there, and those individuals who believe that a new era is beginning, that an old era is ended and that not too much time should be spent in tinkering with it or shoring up the past. It seems clear to me that one era is ended and that another has begun.

PATIENT ACCEPTANCE

For the paramedic to make an important contribution to health services, he or she must be accepted by the patient. Patients who refuse to see paramedics and seek care elsewhere may force physicians to abandon the use of paramedics.

Methods for evaluating patient acceptance have been built into all demonstration projects, and in each case the level of patient acceptance has been high. During the Kansas Demonstration Project, many chronically ill patients preferred the nurse-practitioner, because she gave them more individual attention and psychological support [43, p. 1238]. Plans to study the characteristics of patients asking to leave the nurses' clinic had to be dropped, since only three out of 33 patients transferred [43, p. 1238]. In the Montefiore project, Ford, Seacat and Silver report less than 20 percent of the patients responded negatively to the nurse practitioner [23, p. 1102]. For both obstetrical care and pediatric services, most patients preferred to see both the nurse-practitioner and the physician [23, pp. 1102 - 1103].

Day, Egli, and Silver [16] reported similar acceptance for Colorado Pediatric Nurse-Practitioners utilized in private practice. One group of "old patients" received care both before and after the PNPs' arrival; the "new patients" received care only after the PNPs' arrival (which meant spending less time per visit with the pediatrician). About 92 percent of all patients reported no significant interference with their ability to communicate satisfactorily with the physician. A full 52 percent of new patients, and 22 percent of old patients, actually felt that their ability to communicate with a physician had improved. Ninety-five percent of the mothers were satisfied with their contact with the PNP [16, p. 206].

Several considerations are crucial in assessing and facilitating patient acceptance, including many subjective factors which are hard to analyze. Since the paramedic earns a much lower salary than a physician, he can lower the cost of medical care by assuming some of the tasks usually done by a physician at a higher cost. Such savings, if passed on to the patient, may facilitate patient acceptance. Skinner [62], for example, offered his patients the option of seeing his nurse-practitioner (for well-child care) at a fee lower than he charged for his own time. He reports that many patients accepted the option of lower-cost care and were satisfied with the nurse. The failure of other physicians to price a paramedic visit lower than their own visits may lead some patients to feel exploited, by being seen by the "doctor's assistant." Similarly, indigent people who never pay fees may be sensitive to any apparent degradation in being sent to the "doctor's assistant."

The School of Health of the Oklahoma Medical School and the College of Business Administration at Oklahoma State University are jointly developing a demonstration project to assess the effectiveness of former military independent-duty medical technicians. After a training period of six months, the technician will help provide primary health-care in doctorless rural areas in Oklahoma. In several studies of potential patient acceptance of these technicians, results indicate that the residents of the study communities would use the paramedic 75 percent of the time and would go to existing physician resource in other towns for the remaining 25 percent of their visits [25, 46]. Distance from a physician was the most important variable affecting acceptance [46, p. 2]. Socio-economic variables were not significant although there was some tendency for acceptance to increase with income and education and to decrease with age. (Price was not used as an independent variable.)

ACCEPTANCE BY OTHER PERSONNEL

No formal studies have been done on the acceptance of the paramedic by other health personnel, nor on the importance of such acceptance. Personnel in large institutions have expressed a somewhat ambivalent attitude toward paramedics. While they accept the paramedic, at least in theory, it appears crucial that a physician be actively "in charge," that is, be responsible for, accessible to, and supportive of the paramedics.

There is also evidence that nurses will resist the interposition of this new role between them and the physician. As already discussed, the ANA has been critical of turning nurses into nurse-practitioners. As part of the pediatric nurse-practitioner (PNP) program at Massachusetts General Hospital [7], the PNP is being prepared for such problems, with much time being spent discussing the conflicts of role-orientation. Program personnel also visit the office where the PNP will practice to explain the new role to office employees. Resnik, reporting anecdotes about the nurse-clinician program at Kansas, noted that she had some difficulties obtaining services from social workers [56, p. 7].

Persons trained specifically as physician's assistants might be expected to have less trouble in this area than nurses who have been retrained. Breytspraak and Pondy [11] evaluated eight graduates of the Duke University program, but it is difficult to generalize the results.

It seems reasonable to conclude that acceptance by other health workers will be a difficult problem for the paramedic, at least initially. When the paramedic's role is better understood and more widely accepted, these problems should disappear. Such acceptance is important enough, however, that efforts should be made to isolate the crucial variables and speed the process of acceptance.

## The Economics of Paramedics

PRODUCTIVITY

An implicit assumption behind the concept of the paramedic is that he is an economically viable worker and that his introduction into the health team will lead to an increase in the efficiency with which primary care is delivered. Since this is the critical assumption behind the support for paramedics (and also one critical to their employment by physicians), we now discuss some of the studies that bear on this subject.

Task analysis of physician activities (the best studies are those of pediatric practice) indicate that some physician duties may be assumed by non-physicians with appropriate training. Yankauer, *et al.* [65, p. 524] and Bergman *et al.* [9] determined, for example, that the average pediatrician spends about 50 percent of his time on well-baby care and 30 percent treating minor illnesses—tasks appropriate to paramedics. (A study by Anderson *et al.* of pediatric practice in a small North Carolina town concluded that in rural settings less time was spent on well-baby cases [6]). Silver argues that three pediatric nurse practitioners can replace roughly the time of one pediatrician [60, p. 3]. This estimate reflects a particular distribution of services rendered by the pediatrician and may not include the time a pediatrician must spend supervising. Robert Howard states that physicians using a Duke-trained physician's assistant estimate that they have been able to increase their patient output from 30 to 100 percent [33, p. 415].

Some of these estimates have been verified in practice. For example, in a study in a health station in a low-income housing project when the PNP operated "solo" (a physician came in half a day a week), Silver found that 70 percent of the patients could be completely cared for by the paramedic, and another 11 percent could be cared for after telephone consultation with a physician [61, p. 173].

Schiff *et al.* [57] studied the productivity of a PNP trained in the University of Colorado program. In a private office manned initially by two pediatricians who both had full patient loads, the total number of patients seen increased by 18 percent after the PNP was hired [p. 65]. (The study did not indicate whether the PNP was fully occupied and if the pediatricians worked the same hours.) Although the PNP was paid $7,600 (about 37 percent higher than an ordinary RN), essentially no increase in office overhead occurred and total office income increased by $17,000 [p. 66]. A time analysis showed that on a well-child workup, physician time was reduced from about 14 to four minutes [p. 66]. The PNP took about 30 minutes per well-child workup. The replacement of 10 minutes of physician time by 30 minutes of PNP time agrees well with the overall increase of 36 percent for one physician or 18 percent for two physicians. Since most patients felt their overall care improved, these statistics may represent a decided underestimation of the value of the PNP.

The introduction of the paramedic into the medical team will not necessarily increase the number of patients treated. Physicians, for example, could spend an inordinate amount of time in supervision. Physicians have little training in delegation, and it is unclear how many paramedics can be supervised effectively by one physician. Second, if the physician is very busy, he may choose to keep his case-load constant and decrease the number of hours he practices. In this case his money income will decrease, but his satisfaction may increase since he will have more leisure. If the physician's case-load is kept constant, the number of medical services provided in the community will not increase in the short run. (The time the physician spends with each case may affect quality, however.) In the long run, services may increase, since certain types of practice may become relatively more attractive.

The only data we have where a physician has kept his case-load level is from an unpublished study of a general practitioner who hired a physician's assistant trained at Duke University. Before he hired the assistant, he saw an average of 219 patients per week and spent an average of 9.85 minutes per visit. During the two months after hiring the assistant, he saw 214 patients per week and spent 5.6 minutes per patient; the assistant spent 5.8 minutes per patient and saved the doctor about 43 percent of his time. In the same number of office contact hours per week (36), the doctor could potentially have treated 76 percent more patients. Since he did not, his income has suffered, but his office practice is more attractive and he has more free time.

During the Kansas Nurse Clinic demonstration [42, 26] in which nurse-practitioners treated chronic patients, the overall costs of providing care were reduced in an interesting way. Patients in the experimental group who saw the nurse practitioner were allowed 30-minute visits at about twice the frequency of control patients who had 15-minute physician visits. Since the nurse practitioner costs about ⅜ of the physician, cost of *outpatient* care rose about 70 percent. However, the increased care enabled the experimental group to reduce patient days spent in the hospital by one-third. Since hospitalization formed the bulk of total costs for these chronic patients, overall costs for the control group were reduced from $127 to $99 per patient per year—a reduction of more than 20 percent [42, p. 1239].

The productivity of the paramedic will vary according to the setting in which he is employed. In a large institution or group practice the paramedic can often be employed full time, since he can play a specialized role and capitalize on his training and qualifications. The employment of paramedics may also lead to a lower employment of physicians in institutions. In private practice the opportunities for a paramedic to perform the tasks for which he was trained may be more limited. Some evidence on the placement of paramedics comes from the data on the physician's assistants trained at Duke University. Of the 22 physician's assistants who are involved in patient care, the majority have been hired by large organizations. Specifically, eight are working for physicians in solo practice, three for physicians in group practice, and eleven are working in institutional settings, such as hospitals or prisons.[1]

REIMBURSEMENT POLICIES

Little research has been done on how the paramedic should be reimbursed and on what basis patients should pay for his services. The AMA has strongly endorsed a fee for service concept. Both Skinner [62] and the pediatricians reported in the Schiff [57] study paid their PNP's a salary but charged the PNP patients on a fee-for-service basis.

A more critical problem arises when third parties are introduced. The reimbursement policies can hinder the paramedic's productivity or perhaps even prohibit his introduction. Will Medicaid, Blue Shield, Blue Cross, or Medicare pay for a visit in which the patient sees only a paramedic? In the Kansas program, Medicare would not reimburse the hospital unless the patient was seen by a physician, and Blue Shield, to date, will not pay for obstetrical care by a midwife.

1. Private communication from Dr. Louis Pondy, Duke University.

We presume, however, that payment would be made if a physician "saw" the patient during each visit and signed the chart.

While these rules are laudable attempts to police the system and keep patients away from quacks, they have reduced the efficiency and productivity of paramedics. Hershey argues that legal recognition must be given to the paramedic before these reimbursement problems can be solved [32]. For example, the Kansas experience indicated that a nurse practitioner and patient often had to prolong a visit for 15 to 20 minutes until a physician could see the patient and sign the chart.[2]

## Education and Career Mobility

The whole health-manpower educational system must be restructured to allow health personnel to increase more rapidly than in the past. In this extremely complex issue, both formal education and on-the-job training must be considered together with those for doctors and other allied health personnel. Because of the complexity of the subject and the need for much more research and experimentation, we shall merely sketch the broad outlines of the paramedic issue. (For a more complete discussion of directions in medical education see [17, 19, 21, 45, 51, 63].)

Long-range revamping of medical education will have two major advantages. First, it will enable a more economical use of existing teachers and medical education facilities, since in the short-to-medium range it is difficult to materially affect the supply of these resources. Second, long-range revamping might make health careers more attractive to potential entrants by reducing the costs of education (where feasible), of transferring to a related health career, and of keeping up-to-date in a rapidly changing field. Revamping the system will produce *educational efficiency* and *career mobility*. (These terms are used for convenience, although they do not capture the full scope of the issues. For example, greater career mobility not

2. Private communication from Dr. Waxman, University of Kansas Medical Center.

only encourages new entrants, but also increases the substitutability of supervisory personnel in the short run, thus directly increasing the productivity of a given system.)

In current educational practice in the health professions, the training for each health specialty is completely separate. Especially in introductory courses, medical students, nurse trainees, and pediatrical assistant trainees may all take similar, but separate, courses. Child-behavior courses, for example, are taught by different instructors with different emphases. Since such classes could profitably be larger, there is a direct economic incentive for schools to design common courses wherever feasible. The greatest impediment to such changes is the historic semi-autonomy of each specialty.

Career mobility has four main divisions: vertical, horizontal, geographic, and time. Vertical mobility refers to the ease with which a person can use and augment his knowledge and training to qualify for a "higher" level profession. (In the U.S.S.R. a chief attraction of becoming a feldsher is the increased accessibility to medical school training [58, 59].) Horizontal mobility refers to the ease with which a person may add to his training by changing to a similar health profession at the same level, as in switching from an obstetric to a pediatric assistant. Horizontal mobility also refers to the flexibility in functions which can be built into a profession so that under-utilized assistants in one function can fill vacancies in other functions. Geographic mobility refers to the ease with which a professional may find similar employment in various areas of the country, while time mobility refers to the ease with which he can keep up with technological changes in his specialty. Both geographic and time mobility are closely related to the issue of broadly based general education versus specific apprentice training. The current tendency for the registered nurse to take a four-year B.S. degree from a university rather than the older three-year, hospital-based certificate has ensured the nurse much greater mobility at the cost of an extra year of education and initial on-the-job training. Any change in the educational system inevitably produces changes in the training of health personnel assigned to certain specific tasks. This, of course, raises the issue of measuring how the quality of care is affected.

The quality of care administered by paramedics has already been discussed, but in revamping medical education all allied health personnel must be considered simultaneously.

Perry argues that the whole health field must be subjected to detailed "task analysis," such as has been done extensively in pediatrics [51, p. 110]. To be effective, task analysis should precede any major restructuring of curricula and requirements.

Light [44, p. 79] joins the argument for task analysis, listing it as a prerequisite for the following activities: (1) identifying which components should be taught in the classroom and which on the job; (2) identifying and assigning competency levels for performance; (3) determining which functions can be assigned to a person of given competency; (4) developing more equitable pay schedules; (5) documenting methods for educational equivalency credits; (6) clarifying teaching-learning objectives; and (7) reassessing duties and responsibilities of the specialist in the field.

The task-analysis methods used by industrial engineers in private industry are necessarily slow and cannot be easily implemented in the health field, where the "output," patient health, is difficult to measure. To be effective, such studies must cross professional lines and obtain the full cooperation of the various professional societies such as the AMA. (As noted above, the AMA has issued guidelines for developing new health occupations which seem to strongly support these goals [1], although practical support is more difficult to assess.)

A second prerequisite for developing major curricular changes are university-associated test clinics where the performance of new types of personnel can be evaluated. Current clinics are not adequate for this purpose since the emphasis must be on *testing* rather than *training*; these two functions are probably disparate enough to require separation.

Detailed task analysis and adequate "test laboratories" may provide the tools with which educators and practitioners together may solve the medical-education problem. The general outline of this revision will probably be based on the "core-curriculum" concept by which standardized courses are taken by all personnel. Such standardization enables personnel to use previous training and experience as a basis for upgrading their skills. Thus, certain aspects of the first year or two of the curriculum would be common to medical students, nurses, and paramedics.

Considerable evidence indicates that the most serious obstacle to increasing total health care in the short-to-middle run is the lack of educational facilities. While Morgan [49] and others have suggested shortening medical-school requirements, another solution would seem to be the rapid creation of new medical schools. Because such expansion is extremely difficult, as Estes [20, p. 959] has pointed out, existing facilities must be used as efficiently as possible. The core concept, with its economies of standardization, is one means of increasing efficiency.

A third advantage of the core concept lies in the increased career mobility it affords the allied health worker. Currently, a nurse wishing to become a physician can carry very few of her previous courses into the medical-school program even if the material is quite similar. To facilitate career mobility, considerable pressure is being applied to establish equivalency examinations whereby practical experience can be substituted for formal training. (For further discussion on allied health manpower, see [38, 41, 29, 67].)

A core curriculum, and the career mobility it offers, will perhaps have a greater effect on physician's assistants than on nurse practitioners. With approximately four months of training, the nurse can become a paramedic, a role offering higher pay and more clinical responsibility. However, what kind of advancement is possible for the type of physician's assistant produced by Duke University? Will the student gain any credit towards becoming a physician? Will lack of advancement and the possibility of always being "only an assistant" deter qualified applicants? The core-curriculum idea could enable the paramedic to become a physician in less time than the student entering medical school.

## Legal Issues

A good introduction to legal issues is found in [47], a conference to draft model legislation for physician's assistants. All states can prosecute anyone practicing medicine (diagnosing, treating, performing surgery, or prescribing) without a license. According to the court's clarification of such state laws, most tasks being considered for paramedics would constitute the illegal practice of medicine. For example, some states have explicitly outlawed nurse-midwifery. Legislation was not enacted to outlaw paramedics; rather it stems from an earlier period when the principal concern was protecting the public from quacks. The legislature, if supported by organized medicine, would be open to revising the laws.

Hershey [31, p. 72] believes that in most serious malpractice litigation, the unlicensed therapist is treated as a layman and, thus, automatically considered negligent. Many current practices could be questioned under this interpretation, however, and, if brought to court, the licensing laws would be liberalized quickly. The law tends to confirm current medical practices rather than determine them. Hershey [31, p. 74] also notes that hospitals, which now set the standards for physicians practicing within their confines, could certainly do the same for paramedic personnel, and that private physicians might find such guidelines helpful in setting standards in their private offices.

The principal method for permitting allied health personnel to practice has been to license each group. These licensure laws specify training and the limit of tasks and protect the individual from criminal prosecution and civil malpractice suits. However, they also limit change and introduce rigidity into a system where medical technology is changing rapidly. Legislatures have been unable to revise specific licensure laws rapidly enough to prevent inefficient use of personnel.

The licensure laws make it necessary for an applicant to complete a full, formal training program, no matter what his initial qualifications. For example, for a Licensed Practical Nurse to become a Registered Nurse, she must return to nursing school for the full program and a Registered Nurse must go through four years of medical school and a year of internship to become an MD. Licensure has already introduced into medicine some of the worst facets of the skilled craft unions.

The results of a series of conferences on the legal implications of the Duke physician's assistant program are summarized in the report of a Conference on Legislative Proposals for Physician's Assistants [47]. Conference delegates agreed that the state medical practice acts should be amended and that licensure was a bad way to proceed. Several states, such as Oklahoma, have acts which give the physician the widest possible scope:

> Nothing in this article shall be so construed as to prohibit service rendered by a physician's trained assistant or registered nurse or a licensed practical nurse if such service be rendered under the direct supervision and control of a licensed physician [47, p. 23].

One proposal would modify this wording so that the "act, task, or function is performed in accordance with such rules and regulations as may be promulgated by the Board of Medical Examiners" [p. 38]. A more strict proposal would have the Board of Medical Examiners specify what training is necessary for specified roles and tasks [47, pp. 37 - 38]. A third proposal would have the Board of Medical Examiners consider a petition by an individual physician or institution which specifies the training of a particular employee and the tasks he will perform [47, p. 41].

These proposals differ as to the amount of responsibility given to the physician and as to who shall judge a candidate's qualifications or performance. The AMA supports proposals which would give wide scope to the physician and allow for ". . . growth in the delegation of duties to ancillary health workers" [50, p. 1057]. The AMA proposal would probably lead to more abuse than the others, but it would also increase the number of paramedics and encourage innovation in the way they are used.

To date, state legislatures have taken a wide range of approaches. Colorado requires strict licensure for Child Health Associates, whereas Arizona, Florida, Kansas, and Oklahoma have adopted permissive laws similar to those recommended by the AMA. Curran (as has the AMA [50]) has criticized the Colorado Child Health Associate law:

> This new group is tightly locked into a highly detailed piece of legislation that regulates their activities comprehensively and minutely. It is an excellent model of what should not be done

with any licensed group of professionals, traditional or newly formed [15, p. 1085].

California has recently enacted a law which requires the physician to petition the Board of Medical Examiners to certify a particular applicant to perform specified duties. The future is not at all certain, although there seems to be almost universal agreement that licensure should be avoided.

## Conclusion

We are convinced that expediting the training of paramedics and delegating new tasks to them has much to offer in improving the delivery of medical care in the United States. This program holds out the promise of better medical care for people who cannot currently get care, the promise of a slower rate of increase in medical costs, and the promise of better medical care for many families who find it difficult to see their physician because he is so busy. We feel that sufficient evidence has been collected on these programs to justify major expansion and encouragement.[3]

### REFERENCES

1. AMA Council on Health Manpower: Guidelines for Development of New Health Occupations (adopted by the AMA House of Delegates, Denver, Colorado), December 1969.

2. "AMA Unveils Surprise Plan to Convert R.N. Into Medic," *Amer. J. Nurs.*, vol. 70, no. 4, April 1970, pp. 691 - 693. (Some of these issues are discussed.)

3. "AMA Urges Major New Role for Nurses," *Amer. Med. News*, vol. 13, no. 1, February 9, 1970.

3. The question of what should be public policy toward medical care in general and paramedics in particular is one that has been receiving great attention. Congress has appropriated funds to support the training of allied health personnel, and the executive branch has centralized consideration of these programs and the expenditure of funds for training and evaluation. A book reviewing the programs is: A. Sadler, B. Sadler and A. Bliss, *The Physician's Assistant Today and Tomorrow*, Yale University School of Medicine, 1972.

4. American Academy of Pediatrics, "Suggested Essential Guidelines for the Training of Pediatric Nurse Associates, Pediatric Office Assistants and Pediatric Aides," Comprehensive Health Services, Career Development Issue, vol. 1, no. 3, March 1970.

5. American Nursing Association, *Facts About Nursing*, 1968 edition, 10 Columbus Circle, New York.

6. Anderson, J. H. and Powers, L., "The Pediatric Assignment," *North Carolina Med. J.*, vol. 31, no. 1, January 1970, pp. 1 - 8.

7. Andrews, P., Yankauer, A. and Connelly, Jr., "Changing the Patterns of Ambulatory Pediatric Caretaking—An Action-Oriented Training Program for Nurses," *AJPH*, vol. 60, no. 2, May 1970, pp. 870 - 879.

8. Bane, F., *Physicians for a Growing America*. Report of the Surgeon General's Consultant Group on Medical Education, *U.S. Public Health Service Publication No. 709*, Washington, D.C., U.S. Government Printing Office, 1959.

9. Bergman, A. B., Probstfield, J. L. and Wedgewood, R. L., "Task Identification in Pediatric Practice," *Amer. J. Dis. Children*, vol. 118, September 1969, pp. 459 - 468.

10. Board of Medicine, National Academy of Sciences, "New Members of the Physician's Health Team: Physician's Assistants," Washington, D.C., 1970.

11. Breytspraak, L. and Pondy, L., "Sociological Evaluation of the Physician's Assistants Role Relations," *Group Practice*, vol. 18, no. 3, March 1969, pp. 32 - 41.

12. Collins, M. E. and Bonnyman, G. C., "Physician Assistant and Nurse Associate: A Review," processed, #5 - B, University Court, Charlottesville, Va.

13. Coye, R. and Hansen, M., "The Doctor's Assistant. A Survey of Physicians' Expectations," *JAMA*, vol. 209, July 28, 1969, pp. 529 - 533.

14. Crook, W., "A Practicing Pediatrician Looks at Associates, Assistants, and Aides," *Pediat. Clin. N. Amer.*, vol. 16, no. 4, November 1969.

15. Curran, W., "New Paramedical Personnel—to License or Not to License?" *NEJM*, vol. 282, May 7, 1970, pp. 1085 - 1086.

16. Day, L., Egli, R. and Silver, H., "Acceptance of Pediatric Nurse

Practitioners," *Amer. J. Dis. Children*, vol. 119, March 1970, pp. 203-208.

17. Duncan, B. and Kemp, R., "Joint Education of Medical Students and Allied Health Personnel," *Amer. J. Dis. Children*, vol. 116, November 1968, pp. 499 - 504.

18. Duncan, B., Smith, A. and Silver, H., "Comparison of the Physical Assessment of Children by Pediatric Nurse Practitioners and Pediatricians" (mimeographed), University of Colorado, March 1970.

19. "Educational Programs in Areas Allied with Medicine," *JAMA*, vol. 210, no. 8, November 24, 1969, pp. 1524 - 1529.

20. Estes, E. H., Jr., "The Critical Shortage—Physicians and Supporting Personnel," *Ann. Intern. Med.*, vol. 69, no. 5, November 1968, pp. 957 - 962.

21. Estes, E. H., Jr., "Medical Education—Reformation or Revolution," *Amer. J. Med. Sci.*, vol. 256, December 1968, pp. 335 - 339.

22. Fein, R., *The Doctor Shortage: An Economic Diagnosis*, Washington, D.C., Brookings Institution, 1967.

23. Ford, F., Seacat, M. and Silver, G., "The Relative Roles of the Public Health Nurse and the Physician in Prenatal and Infant Supervision," *AJPH*, vol. 56, no. 7, July 1966, pp. 1097 - 1103.

24. Forgotson, E. H. and Forgotson, J., "Innovations and Experiments in Uses of Health Manpower," *Medical Care*, vol. 8, January, February 1970, pp. 3 -14.

25. Fry, F., "A Study of the Acceptability of the former Military Independent Duty Corpsman as a Medical Resource in Rural Communities," unpublished Master's Thesis, Oklahoma State University, May 1970.

26. Gerber, A., "Comments on Ambulatory Care in Nurse Clinics," *NEJM*, vol. 278, no. 13, March 1968, p. 737.

27. Ginzberg, E., "Facts and Fancies About Medical Care," *AJPH*, vol. 69, no. 5, May 1969, pp. 785 - 794.

28. Ginzberg, E., "Physician Shortage Reconsidered," *NEJM*, vol. 275, no. 2, July 14, 1966, pp. 85 - 87.

29. Greenfield, H. and Brown, C., "Allied Health Manpower: Trends and Prospects," Columbia University Press, 1969.

30. Hansen, W. L., "Shortages and Investment in Health Manpower," *The Economics of Health and Medical Care*, The University of Michigan, 1964, pp. 75 - 91.

31. Hershey, N., "An Alternative to Mandatory Licensing of Health Professionals," *Hosp. Progress*, vol. 50, March 1969, pp. 71 -74.

32. Hershey, N., "Patient Free Choice: A Relative Concept for the Insured Patient," *The Insurance Law Journal*, no. 533, February 1969, pp. 71 - 80.

33. Howard, D. R., "The Physician's Assistant," *Kansas Med. Soc. J.*, vol. VXV, no. 10, October 1969, pp. 411 - 416.

34. Howard, D. R. and Fasser, C. E., "A Progress Report on Duke University's Physician's Assistant Program," *Hosp. Progress*, vol. 51, February 1970, pp. 49 - 55.

35. Howard, Ernest B., "Organized Medicine," The AMA, Lowell Lecture, Boston University Medical School, January 6, 1970. (As reported in 24 above.)

36. Kadish, J. and Long, J., "The Training of Physician Assistants: Status and Issues," *JAMA*, vol. 212, no. 6, May 11, 1970, pp. 1047 - 1051.

37. Kaufmann, C., "How They Train Midwives at Columbia," *Resident Physician*, vol. 14, February 1968, pp. 96 - 101.

38. Kissick, W., "Effective Utilization: The Critical Factor in Health Manpower," *AJPH*, vol. 58, no. 1, January 1968, pp. 23 - 29.

39. Knowles, J. H., "The Quality and Quantity of Medical Manpower: A Review of Medicine's Current Efforts," *J. Med. Ed.*, vol. 44, February 1969.

40. Ledney, D., "Nurse-Midwives: Can They Fill the OB Gap?" *RN*, January 1970, pp. 38 - 45.

41. Levine, H., "Career Ladders and Equivalency Examinations: What Does It All Mean?" *Amer. J. Med. Technol.*, vol. 35, no. 11, November 1969, pp. 714 - 720.

42. Lewis, C. and Resnik, B., "Nurse Clinics and Progressive Ambulatory Patient Care," *NEJM*, vol. 277, December 7, 1967, pp. 1236 - 1241.

43. Lewis, C., Resnik, B., Schmidt, G. and Waxman, D., "Activities, Events and Outcomes in Ambulatory Patient Care," *NEJM*, vol. 280, no. 12, March 20, 1969, pp. 645 - 649.

44. Light, I., "Growth and Development of New Allied Health Fields," *Amer. J. Med. Technol.*, vol. 36, no. 2, February 1970, pp. 75 - 83.

45. "Medical Education in the U.S.: Education Programs in Areas Allied to Medicine," *JAMA*, vol. 206, no. 9, November 25, 1968, pp. 2053 - 2058.

46. Mingo, K. and Fry, F., "An Analysis of the Variables Related to the Acceptance of Physician's Assistants in Doctorless Rural Communities," working paper, Oklahoma State University, 1970.

47. "Model Legislation Project for Physician's Assistants" (mimeographed), Department of Community Health Services, Duke University, June 30, 1970.

48. Montgomery, B., Report to the Bd. of Trustees—AMA Position Statement on Nursing, adopted by the House of Delegates, June 1970.

49. Morgan, R., "Physician Assistants: Their Role in Medicine in the Years Ahead," *J. Maine Med. Assoc.*, vol. 59, no. 11, November 1968, pp. 219 - 223.

50. "Of Physician Assistants: Editorial," *JAMA*, vol. 212, May 11, 1970, p. 1057.

51. Perry, J., "Career Mobility in Allied Health Education," *JAMA*, vol. 210, no. 1, October 6, 1969, pp. 107 - 110.

52. Professional Activities Branch, HEW, "Selected Training Programs for Physician Support Personnel," (mimeographed pamphlet).

53. *Report of the AAMC Task Force on Physician's Assistant Programs*, Association of American Medical Colleges, Washington, D.C., February 1970.

54. *Report of the Ad Hoc Committee on Allied Health Professionals*, American Society of Internal Medicine, San Francisco, January 1970.

55. *Report of the National Advisory Commission on Health Manpower*, Washington, D.C., vol. 1 and 2, 1968.

56. Resnik, B. A., "The Nursing Clinic: An Experiment in Ambulatory Patient Care" (mimeographed), presented to the Kansas Nursing Assoc.

57. Schiff, D., Fraser, C. and Walters, H., "The Pediatric Nurse Practitioner in the Office of Pediatricians in Private Practice," *Pediatrics*, vol. 44, no. 1, July 1969, pp. 62 - 68.

58. Sidel, V. W., "Feldshers and Feldsherism," *NEJM*, vol. 278, no. 17, April 25, 1968, pp. 934 - 939.

59. Sidel, V. W., "Feldshers and Feldsherism," *NEJM*, vol. 278, no. 18, May 2, 1968, pp. 987 - 992.

60. Silver, H., "New Patterns of Personnel for Children's Services. A Blueprint for Child Health Care for the Next Decade," paper presented at 38th Annual Meeting of the Amer. College of Pediatrics, October 18, 1969.

61. Silver, H. and Hecker, S., "The Pediatric Nurse Practitioner and the Child Health Associate," *J. Med. Edu.*, vol. 45, March 1970, pp. 171 - 176.

62. Skinner, A., "Parental Acceptance of Delegated Pediatric Services," *Pediatrics*, vol. 41, May 1968, pp. 1003 - 1004.

63. Stead, E., Jr., "Educational Programs and Manpower," *Bull. N. Y. Acad. Med.*, vol. 44, no. 2, February 1968, pp. 204 - 213.

64. Stitham, L., "Physician's Assistants: More Problems or Less?" *J. Maine Med. Assoc.*, vol. 59, November 1968, pp. 225 - 226.

65. Yankauer, A., Connelly, J. P. and Feldman, J. J., "Pediatric Practices in the United States," *Pediatrics* (Supplement), vol. 45, February 1970, pp. 521 - 554.

66. Yankauer, A., Connelly, J. P. and Feldman, J., "A Survey of Allied Health Worker Utilization in Pediatric Practice in Massachusetts and the U.S.," *Pediatrics*, vol. 42, no. 5, November 1968, pp. 733 - 742.

67. Zimmerman, T., "Laddering and Latticing: Trends in Allied Health," *Amer. J. Occup. Ther.*, vol. 24, no. 2, March 1970, pp. 102 - 105.

# III

# Education

Larry D. Singell *is associate professor of economics at the University of Colorado in Boulder. He attended Eastern Nazarene College for his B.A., and received his M.A. and Ph.D. in economics from Wayne State University. His published research has dealt with human resource problems relating to the urban environment, and he has served as a consultant to a variety of government agencies, including the National Institutes of Education. Dr. Singell is currently editing three volumes of the forthcoming* Collected Papers of Kenneth E. Boulding.

Wesley J. Yordon *is professor of economics at the University of Colorado in Boulder. A native of Plainfield, New Jersey, he attended Wesleyan University and the University of Colorado, receiving his B.A.* magna cum laude *from the latter in 1956. Harvard university awarded him the Ph.D. in economics in 1960. He has been teaching at the University of Colorado since 1959, with time out to serve as Fulbright Lecturer in Argentina (1963) and Mexico (1965 - 66). Among his extra - curricular activities has been a term as president of the Boulder Valley public school system. Dr. Yordon's published research includes considerable work on the use of prices in economic decision-making.*

# 4

# Incentives for More Efficient Education: The Development of a Model

## LARRY D. SINGELL AND
## WESLEY J. YORDON

The purpose of this paper is to develop a testable incentive model for achieving efficiency in public education. The particular model is one that relies on cash rewards to teachers (and administrators) who are responsible for raising a given measure of educational output such as reading scores or math scores. The model is designed to overcome the dominance of socio-economic status (SES) over academic achievement.

The topic is one that involves strong opinions and powerful emotions. Accordingly, we enter some *caveats* at this point so as to avoid misunderstandings:

1. The model is an experimental one and is not offered as a solution to the nation's educational problems.
2. It is one of several possible models that rely upon cash. Alternatives that we have proposed elsewhere include cash rewards to pupils and parents.[1]
3. We do not argue here that cash incentives are necessarily superior to other types of incentives.
4. We do not, in this paper, try to deal with the ethical issues involved in experimenting with children or other humans.

1. See Larry D. Singell and Wesley J. Yordon, "Alternative Incentive Models for Education," Final Report submitted to New York University and U.S. Department of Health, Education and Welfare, under Contract HEW-OS-69-94, September 1, 1970.

We recognize, however, that these are issues of considerable importance.

Our plan is to discuss briefly some of the literature on the
production of education, with emphasis on the problem of
relating educational inputs to outputs. Then, since most existing studies suffer from the ambiguities characteristic of a cross-
sectional approach, we shall offer the results of a longitudinal
pilot study conducted by us in Boulder, Colorado. Then, given
the implications of the pilot study, we develop our proposal
for an experimental program.

## The Problem of Efficiency in Public Education

A significant and increasing number of research efforts relating
to the production of education have reached the conclusion
of the now famous "Coleman Report" that: "socio-economic
factors have a strong relation to academic achievement. When
these factors are statistically controlled, however, it appears
that differences between schools account for only a small fraction of differences in pupil achievement."[2]

The validity of these findings is obviously of critical importance. Policies based on the proposition that what goes on
inside the classroom has little or no effect on pupil achievement
can be socially deleterious if the proposition is, in fact, based
on faulty reasoning or biased statistical evidence. This accounts
for the considerable discussion that has occurred about

2. James S. Coleman, *et al.*, *Equality of Educational Opportunity*, Washington: U.S. Government Printing Offices (1966), p. 21f. The Coleman Report
has been attacked for numerous methodological faults, and critics have demonstrated that the same data may be used to show contradictory results. For
the most systematic criticism see Samuel Bowles and Henry Levin, "The
Determinants of Scholastic Achievement: An Appraisal of some Recent Evidence," *The Journal of Human Resources*, III (Winter, 1968), pp. 3-24. Bowles
and Levin point out: "By no means do we wish to suggest that the actual
relations are the opposite of what the Coleman Report concludes or that further
research will not substantiate some of the Report's findings; but until better
evidence is found, we will have to remain agnostic about which relationships
prevail" (p. 23). See also S. Bowles and H. Levin, "More on Multicollinearity
and the Effectiveness of Schools," *The Journal of Human Resources*, Vol.
III (Summer, 1968), pp. 393 - 400 and S. Bowles and H. Levin, "Towards
Equality of Educational Opportunity," *Harvard Educational Review*, Vol.
38 (Winter, 1968), pp. 89 - 99.

Coleman's statistical methodology and data base. However, other approaches, using other data bases, have led to a similar conclusion.

Thomas Ribich, utilizing the Project Talent data, found that if socio-economic class is held constant, increased expenditure per pupil had almost no effect on pupil performance as measured by a diverse battery of tests.[3] In fact, for both low- and high-status pupils a *doubling* of *expenditure* per pupil (from $200—$300 to $400—$500) was associated with an improvement of only one-quarter of a grade level. Furthermore, socio-economic class is the major variable in determining school outcomes. Thus, lower-class pupils in the *most* expensive schools were on the average a grade and one-half below the high-status pupils in the *lowest* expenditure districts. While a host of factors may explain this phenomenon it is quite clear, on the basis of this data, that increasing expenditure or "doing more of the same" cannot be relied upon to improve educational outcome.

But even when one examines programs that do not "do more of the same," the results are not encouraging. For example, Burton Weisbrod in examining the cost-benefit ratios of a dropout-prevention program concluded that on economic grounds saving dropouts did not pay! Weisbrod estimated that each rescued dropout would earn an average of $3,427 more over his lifetime (present discounted value) but that the reduction in the dropout rate, as a result of the program, was so low that each rescue cost $8,200.[4]

Similarly, attempts have been made to estimate the cost

3. See Thomas I. Ribich, *Education and Poverty*, Brookings Institution, Washington, D.C. (1968), p. 117. For a description on the methodology of the study see, John C. Flanagan and others, *Designing the Study*, Technical Report to U.S. Office of Education, Cooperative Research Project 566 (University of Pittsburgh, Project Talent Office, 1966). See also: Flanagan and others, *Studies of the American High School*, Technical Report to U.S. Office of Education, Cooperative Research Project 226 (University of Pittsburgh, Project Talent Office, 1962); Flanagan and others, *The American High School Student*, Technical Report to U.S. Office of Education, Cooperative Research Project 635 (University of Pittsburgh, Project Talent Office, 1964).

4. Burton A. Weisbrod, "Preventing High School Dropouts," in Robert Dorfman (ed.), *Measuring Benefits of Government Investments*, Brookings Institution (1965), pp. 117-149.

and returns of various compensatory education efforts. Although it is questionable whether these "pilot" projects are truly representative of what might occur under broadly based programs, it is interesting to note that, at best, success is problematical. One large-scale compensatory educational experiment which utilized numerous measures for evaluation was the Higher Horizons Program in New York City.[5] This program focused on third- and seventh-grade pupils by providing special services including remedial reading, extra counseling of students and parents, cultural activities, and specially tailored curriculum changes—all this backed up by additional teachers and extra professional staff. Services were received by 64,075 pupils at a cost of approximately $61 per student per year. While a small gain in standardized achievement test scores was made by the Higher Horizons group as compared with a control group who did not have the benefit of the additional services (roughly the gain was only three percent a year more expressed in yearly equivalents) other evidence is mixed. For example, after two years, differences in IQ between the Higher Horizons and the control group were small and went in both directions, and an index designed to measure attitude with regard to education devised by the Higher Horizons research team showed no significant difference between the control and experimental group.

Disaggregated research efforts have produced results that are equally disturbing. In one of the most extensive studies, Jesse Burkhead examined the relationship of inputs to outputs in the high schools of several large cities.[6] This study utilized several alternative measures of output including students employed, post-high school educational intentions, percent dropouts and various test scores. The study's major conclusions were:

1. The socio-economic, or out-of-school variables, are far more significant in determining differences in school out-

5. The discussion of this project draws on the work of Thomas Ribich, *op. cit.*, pp. 61-78.

6. Jesse Burkhead, *Input and Output in Large-City Schools*, Syracuse: Syracuse University Press (1967).

puts than the in-school variables. In fact, the typical pattern that emerged was if socio-economic class was forced to enter the equation first, all other school input or process variables were statistically insignificant.

2. Neither class size nor teacher man-years per student appear to be important in producing different educational outcomes although the variation within cities may not have been sufficient to reveal systematic differences.

3. While none of the input variables are highly significant, some inputs appear important for some outputs but not for others. In Chicago, for example, newer buildings were associated with fewer school dropouts, but they had no influence on 11th grade reading scores.

4. Teacher experience is an important variable, particularly by its impact on reading scores, and it tends to be more important than class size or the formal education of the teacher.

5. Size of the school is not a consistently important variable.

The above merely highlights some of the existing analysis of input-output relationships in the educational industry.[7] Alexander Mood summarizes the basic difficulty encountered in research efforts of this type by noting:

> Student achievement correlates with almost any school attributes and it is no trick to build up a set of attributes which generate a sizeable correlation. The same can be done with home attributes or with community attributes. When one tries to control one set in order to assess the effect of another set he finds he has overcontrolled and the sought after effect is very small—vastly smaller than what it would be without the control.

Thus, Mood concludes:

> All we can say about this matter at the present time is the following: children from well-to-do, well-educated families tend to get higher

7. A very excellent, as well as the most recent summary and critique of these studies may be found in James W. Guthrie, "A Survey of School Effectiveness Studies," Chap. 2 in *Do Teachers Make a Difference*, A Report on Recent Research on Pupil Achievement, U.S. Department of Health, Education and Welfare, Office of Education, U.S. Government Printing Office, Washington, D.C. (1970).

achievement scores; children having higher-salaried teachers tend to get higher achievement scores; higher-salaried teachers tend to be found in well-to-do school districts; there is insufficient evidence to determine how much of the higher achievement should be attributed to the home and how much to the teachers.

These same observations apply as well to other teacher characteristics. Thus, with respect to experience, experienced teachers develop seniority and hence some choice about where they teach; they tend to gravitate to the comfortable suburbs; hence one finds good association between student achievement and teacher experience. How much of the higher achievement should be attributed to teacher experience? The present rudimentary state of our knowledge permits us to make no reasonable estimate of it.[8]

There is reason to believe that the research efforts described above have been designed in such a manner that they fail to disclose the relationships sought for. Several reasons may be offered. First, outputs (achievement test scores) in a given grade level have been related only to inputs in that grade level,[9] thus ignoring the fact that achievement levels in any grade are likely to be a function of resource allocations previous to that grade. By utilizing cross-sectional data, these studies overlook not only the influence of previous resource allocations, but the related problem of migration. A significant part of the pupil population (in some large city schools as high as 100 percent) change schools every year. It is a mistake to relate achievement scores of these migrant pupils to the resource allocations patterns existing in the schools in which they are examined.

Second, existing studies have all utilized average scores for a particular school or school district as a measure of output. The use of means or averages clouds a considerable amount of variance which *in fact may be the essence of the problem*. That is, resource allocation patterns in a particular school/school district may affect some youths favorably while af-

8. *Ibid.*, A. M. Mood, "Do Teachers Make a Difference?"

9. For example, the Burkhead Study used test scores in the 11th grade as the dependent variable while the independent variables were inputs used at that grade level. Cf: Burkhead, *op. cit.*

fecting others adversely.[10] Not only will the use of means "wash out" this effect, but the level of aggregation may make the results less meaningful from an administrative or policy point of view. If resource allocation decisions are made at the school-building level, then the input-output relationship within rather than across schools is the relevant one.

Third, to the extent that an implicit allocation process operates in which the better (*i.e.*, most capable, experienced or more successful) teachers in a given system move from lower to upper socio-economic class schools or pupils, then that which has been attributed to socio-economic class may actually be a result of different patterns of resource allocation. Such a pattern may not stem from explicit administrative decisions, yet it may be quite important. The existence of the effect has been well documented by Patricia Sexton in her study of education in a large city.[11]

In addition to these conceptual issues, several statistical-methodological ones may exist. A major problem comes from the use of the multiple coefficient of determination[12] (or additions to $R^2$) and regression coefficients[13] as a reflector of the relative importance of a specific variable for policy purposes. If the real policy question is, which use of the scarce item (for example, dollars in the budget) yields the largest increment in output (for example, achievement scores), then the $R^2$ criterion, or the size and significance of the regression coefficient are inadequate considerations.

If, however, policy is to be based on relative cost, then the critical information is the relative cost of various inputs associated with changing output by a specified amount. Hence,

10. There are several problems with the use of means or averages. First, they may not really measure well what is intended. For example, average of teacher experience may be identical in two schools, one having 10 teachers with 20 years experience and 30 with none, the other having 40 teachers with five years experience. In addition, variance in pupil response could be significant even though means are identical.

11. Patricia Cayo Sexton, *Education and Income*, New York: Viking Press (1964).

12. Coleman, *op. cit.*

13. Burkhead, *op. cit.*

properly scaled regression coefficients will be a useful focus of attention. Cost, in terms of dollars, would be the most straightforward scaling device, but time, political consensus, or other variables could also be experimented with.

In essence what has been suggested above is that there may be some reason to attempt a more disaggregated study of input-output relationships which concentrates on individual students and particular inputs associated with those students in a longitudinal context.

## The Pilot Study

We tried to overcome some of the difficulties of aggregated cross-sectional analysis by designing a study which relates individual pupil-achievement scores to specific difference in teacher inputs, the social status of pupils, and a rough measure of pupils' innate endowment. The sample consisted of 100 male pupils (drawn from 22 fourth-grade classes in seven different schools) who had been continuously enrolled in Boulder Valley Public Schools since kindergarten. Included were eight pupils from poverty-status families, eight Spanish-surnamed pupils,[14] and 87 middle-class Anglo pupils. The achievement scores in mathematics and reading were collected for these 100 students for the first through the fourth grades along with their reading-readiness scores from kindergarten. Teacher inputs consisted of age, experience, and earned graduate credits. At each grade level, the teacher characteristics of both the current and previous grade levels were considered. Social-status variables used were poverty status (or not)[15] and Spanish-surnamed (or not). We do not, of course, have a pure measure of innate endowment. The variable used at the first-grade level was the kindergarten reading-readiness score. The authors of this test indicate that performance is a function of both intelligence and home background; hence, we used these scores as

14. In three of the eight cases the pupil had a Spanish surname and came from a poor household.
15. The poverty variable was supplied by the Title I Office. Criteria were: Title I eligibility, welfare status, or income just above the borderline.

a surrogate measure of innate endowment and socio-economic class. It is very likely that it is a significantly more consistent measure of the latter, but it, of course, cannot be independent of the former.

We are aware of both the limited sample size and the aggregated nature of teacher characteristics, but time constraints forced these limitations upon us. The major purpose for the pilot study was to develop some propositions about input-output relationships that could be utilized and tested in experimental incentive programs. A complete description of the study can be found in the final report of our project.[16]

> Proposition 1: *The educational system is clearly more responsive and conventional inputs are more effective with higher-achieving students. This results in a widening gap between higher and lower achievers as grade levels advance.*

A commonly held view of the educational industry is that it is aimed at the average and middle-class student. After finding a somewhat weak relationship between conventional inputs and achievement scores for the total sample of pupils, we were interested in testing this hypothesis. Since the designers of the reading-readiness exams had demonstrated that these scores reflected some combination of native intelligence and home environment, we used these scores to eliminate the upper and lower 10 percent of the distribution. The remaining students could be characterized as "middle-class, average students." The regression results, however, were somewhat disquieting. They indicated that, if anything, conventional teacher inputs had a smaller and less statistically significant impact on this group than on the total sample.

Moreover, when we divided our sample into those above and below the average reading-readiness groups we discovered, for example, that at the first-grade level, the impact of teacher experience on mathematics achievement for the above-average group was over twice as great as for the below-average group, and the comparable impact of graduate credit

16. Singell and Yordon, *op. cit.*

was over three times greater. A smaller but similar disparity was found in regard to reading achievement. Furthermore, the variation in reading achievement in the first grade associated with reading readiness was three times greater for the above-average reading-readiness group than for those below average. It is difficult to disentangle how much of this results from teachers putting more of their energies into aiding the higher-achieving student and how much is a result of socio-economic class influences outside the school. (Poverty status and Spanish-surnames were allowed to enter the equation, but were not statistically significant in the first grade.) Of course, it is also quite possible that the historical bias in education of concentrating on the intellectually and socially elite is still unconsciously (or consciously) pursued in the sense that teacher preparation is geared to the needs of the achieving student. What appears to the teacher to be a lack of motivation or intellectual capability on the part of the student may be due fundamentally to a very specialized training on the part of the teacher.

These results do suggest, however, that even if one were to disaggregate and isolate what lies behind the variables of experience and graduate credit, greater, and/or perhaps restructured quantities of conventional inputs might be required for achieving a given improvement in the educational outcomes for lower-achieving and lower socio-economic class students.

> Proposition 2: *Test scores in reading are a poor choice as a surrogate measure of achievement when examining the impact of the teacher on student performance because the cultural bias in the test results in failure to disclose relationships which actually exist.*

This proposition is based largely on our findings that the relationships between the conventional inputs and achievement in mathematics were far more consistent and significant than those for reading. For example, only a handful of the regression coefficients measuring the impact of the conventional inputs on achievement scores in mathematics were statistically insignificant, but approximately two-thirds of these regression coefficients were statistically insignificant in the reading equations. In addition, the coefficients of multiple correlation were on the average 15 percent higher and the standard error of the estimates were on the average 20 percent lower in the mathematics equations as compared to the reading equations.

Perhaps the teaching of reading is more of an art than a "science," although the graduate credit earned by the teacher was the most consistently statistically significant variable in the reading equations. However, it can be argued that the conventional inputs had less measured impact because the opportunity for cultural bias to have an effect is greater in the teaching and testing of reading than in mathematics. We received a strong impression of the latter, but cannot offer conclusive proof that this is so.

Proposition 3: *After kindergarten, the age of the teacher has a consistently negative influence on educational outcomes.*

While a complete explanation of this phenomenon must await a more disaggregated study of this variable, several hypotheses may be offered. First, younger teachers may have received better or more modern training. That is, older teachers may not have adjusted well to the "new math." However, since no new changes have taken place in the teaching of reading which can be compared with the new math (in the last five years) and this negative relationship is also present in reading, some additional explanation is necessary. (It is interesting to note here that older teachers also appear to have a more adverse effect on the students with above-average reading readiness than those with below-average reading readiness.) Our data is not detailed enough and the sample size was too small (and very likely the problem is too complex) for us to offer such additional explanations. We were impressed, however, with the fact that when we isolated students with very young teachers they tended to show greater changes in achievement scores. Thus, for example, of the 64 teachers in our sample, 14 were 30 years of age or younger and these younger teachers had an average of 4.9 years of teaching experience. (The average age of all teachers in the sample was 42.7 years and average experience was 14.3 years). The students who were enrolled in the classes of these 14 younger teachers were 17 percent above the sample mean in the fourth-grade composite achievement score. To what extent this is due to greater excitement, empathy, energy or better training, we cannot be sure.

Proposition 4: *If a student comes from a poor family, an additional learning handicap is imposed if he attends a school with other poor children.*

Two of the schools used in the sample had constituent populations that were lower in socio-economic class than the average for the total sample. When a "dummy variable" was entered for these two schools it was consistently statistically significant. The coefficient of the dummy variable suggested that if teacher age, experience and graduate credit were "held constant," the students from these two schools would be from one-third to one-quarter of a grade level below the average in the first grade and this gap would increase throughout the period of our sample observations. On the basis of the composite score in the fourth grade, students from these two schools were about three-quarters of a grade below the mean.

There are several possible explanations of this phenomenon which cannot be completely disentangled from our data. While the teachers in these two schools were slightly older than average (less than a year) they were also more experienced (13 percent more) and had more graduate training (four percent more). Since the average differences in teacher characteristics in each case were too small to account for the difference in scores, we were led to believe, although it cannot be proved conclusively, that this is more a "peer-group" phenomenon than a "teacher-difference" phenomenon.

Proposition 5: *When socio-economic class is held constant, the characteristics of the first teachers a student has are*

> *the most consistent predictors of the student's later academic achievement.*

One of the most consistent and interesting patterns that emerged from our pilot study is that the age, experience and graduate credit of the first-grade teachers were predominantly the statistically significant variables in explaining the second-, third- and fourth-grade achievement scores in both mathematics and reading. An alternative way of looking at this phenomenon is that, except for groups with above-average reading-readiness scores, third-grade teacher characteristics were *never* statistically significant and only a handful of the regression coefficients for second-grade teacher characteristics entered the equation as statistically significant.

One reaction to this might be that this is purely spurious because the characteristics of the first teachers a student has are likely to be highly related to the characteristics of future teachers; hence, the first-grade characteristics are really a surrogate measure of later teacher inputs. However, when we removed the first-grade characteristics from the equations, second- and third-grade characteristics were still statistically insignificant. The only exception to this was with higher-achieving (above-average reading-readiness) students, where conventional teacher inputs were generally statistically significant.

Thus, we have a strong feeling from examining the data that the first learning experience the student has shapes, in some fundamental way, his future achievement. While future teacher inputs may modify this they may have to be quite dramatic before a noticeable effect appears. Although we could isolate several second- and third-grade teachers who seemed to have a more significant impact on student performance than the average, the number of observations was too small to relate these differences systematically to the teacher characteristics we utilized. While we are convinced that these teacher characteristics do make a difference, the relationship is far too complex to be captured by our highly aggregated model and our small sample. In fact, an area for future research which may

yield some real insight into the educational process would
be to closely examine these "later" teachers who do have some
widespread and significant impact.

  Proposition 6: *Differences in achievement scores by students with differing cultural backgrounds (race or class)
  are distinctly affected by the testing devices utilized. The
  degree of "cultural bias" in the testing is so irregular
  that if resource-allocation decisions were based on them,
  misallocation would be inevitable.*

Since students with Spanish surnames scored on the average
20 percent below the total sample average in reading readiness,
it was anticipated that this variable would be a significant
factor in predicting reading achievement at other grade levels.
However, when these regressions were calculated, the significance of this variable was highly irregular. In the first grade
the coefficient was not significantly different from zero, but
in the second grade the same pupils scored on the average
three-quarters of a grade level below the total sample mean
and the Spanish-surnamed variable was significant (at the one
percent level). In the third and fourth grades, once again, the
coefficients were not significantly different from zero.

  The same kind of irregularity was encountered with the
poverty-status variable. This was statistically insignificant from
kindergarten through third grade, but became highly significant in the fourth grade. Since the school system used Met-
ropolitan Achievement Tests to measure achievement in
grades one through three and Iowa Achievement Exams in
grade four it seems quite probable that this change is the result
of a change in tests rather than a change in ability.

  It is clear to us from these findings that the devices for
assessing achievement did not discriminate achievement from
cultural homogeneity in any systematic way. If the extent to
which the environment of poverty or cultural differences are
a handicap in learning is a function of which achievement
exams were used to evaluate learning achievement, then
resource-allocation decisions cannot be based on them. In
addition, if incentive systems are based on changes in achieve-

ment levels, explicit account has to be taken of the cultural bias which exists in the assessment instruments.

## A Proposal for Experimentation

Two of the most significant findings from the pilot study were the pervasive impact of early teachers and the apparent "peer-group" effect which appeared when poverty-status students were mixed with middle-class students in the same learning environment. Thus, we feel that an experimental incentive system incorporating these two factors may have a great deal of promise both for understanding the educational process and for creating equality of educational opportunity.

We propose an experimental program in which 1,000 first-grade children who had below-average reading-readiness scores in kindergarten be transferred to middle-class schools for the first grade. This program is designed with a city of between 500 thousand and one million population as a base, but the scale can be adjusted proportionately for a smaller city or region. The selection of 1,000 students would provide an adequate sample for the general evaluation of the effectiveness of the program. However, the program could easily involve only 100 students and still yield considerable insight.

In an effort to test the peer-group phenomenon, a "benign quota" must be adhered to in this transfer process. The most frequent (the modal) size elementary school is 600 pupils, with approximately 100 first-grade students. In the light of this, we suggest that approximately 20 pupils be transferred to each of 50 middle-class elementary schools. If the 20 students to be transferred can be selected from the same neighborhood, this will minimize the transportation cost and maintain to some extent the valuable aspects of the "neighborhood" school. That is, students who interact together in the neighborhood would also attend the same school.

What incentives to experiment should be offered to government? To begin with, it is helpful to estimate the expenditures that state, local, and federal governments could make, as well as the results necessary for this system to "pay for itself" in the sense of having a benefit-cost ratio greater than one. Thomas Ribich has estimated the value of an additional year of elementary schooling, in terms of the present discounted value of future income, as $2,410.[17] If we assume the conservative income tax rates of 15 percent for the federal government and five percent for state and local governments, then the expected present discounted value of tax revenues due to each extra year of school per pupil is $480. In addition, if the school system does not adequately provide for the needs of lower-status youth, additional social costs of delinquency, welfare costs and intergenerational effects might be considerable, not to mention the psychic costs to the individual. Hence, this expected $480 gain per student per grade could be treated as a *minimum* gain to all units of government for investing in an additional year of elementary training.

It might be noted here that if perfect capital markets existed, a hypothetical student or his family could pay up to $2,410 in taxes to support the schools and, if the schools expanded his achievement levels by at least one year, this would be a "good investment." The fact that society spends much less gives some indication of under-investment in education. Thus, Weisbrod estimates the rate of return to grade-school education to be over 50 percent when the option demand is considered, and over 35 percent without it. It goes without saying that this is a substantially higher rate of return than other investment options in society.[18]

With respect to the state and local governments it could be argued that migration will lead states and localities not to expect an additional tax return to accrue to them. While this is clearly a problem, the fact that the gains are considerably understated may mean that states may and should be willing to spend this additional amount even when discounting for migration. To the extent that this is not so, block grants or revenue-sharing schemes may have to be devised to handle

17. Ribich, *op. cit.*, p. 71.
18. B. A. Weisbrod, "Education and Investment in Human Capital," *Journal of Political Economy*, Vol. 70, No. 5, part 2, supplement (1962), pp. 106-123.

this problem. This problem, however, is beyond the scope of this study.

## Incentives for the Individual School

We will assume in the following that the expenditures per pupil at the elementary level will be $800 when this program is attempted. The data from our Boulder Valley School sample suggests that students who start first grade with below-average reading-readiness scores finish first grade on the average at one-third below grade level. Hence, we propose that the school to which these students transfer receive $800 per pupil if these students finish the first grade at two-thirds the mean composite achievement score (weighting equally reading and mathematics). This $800 would be shifted from the budget of the school which would ordinarily serve the transferred student. Assuming constant returns to scale (which seems realistic over this range), this should work no hardship on the poverty-status school. If students perform better than the two-thirds of a grade level, the receiving school would receive additional funds. We propose the schedule of per-student payments as shown in Table 4.1.

TABLE 4.1. *Schedule of Per-Pupil Payments to School Based on Performance in Changing Scores of Transfer Students*

| Composite Score in Grade Equivalent | Payments per Pupil |
|---|---|
| .67 to .99 | $ 800 |
| 1.00 to 1.29 | 1000 |
| 1.30 and above | 1200 |

It is important to note that the school receiving the low-status students takes no risk. That is, it receives their average cost no matter how well the transferred students perform. Our results from the pilot study suggest these students may achieve at, or close to, grade level simply because of the "peer-group effect." Based on the assumed formula used in the table above, the average school serving 20 transfer students would receive an additional $4,000 above cost if students should be brought up to grade level. If the school should increase scores above the 1.3 grade level it would receive $8,000 above its normal cost. That is, it would receive the full expected present discounted value of increased tax revenues (less $80.00 per pupil for administrative costs that will be discussed later) that would result from changing the achievement of students by one full grade level.

How should this potential gain of $8,000 be handled? It is here that the question of incentives enters. The critical incentives in our experiment will be those relating to the administrators and teachers in the middle class school. We shall assume that the parents of the students desire improvement and, if teachers are effective with the students, that students will be motivated to achieve.[19] Therefore, we propose that one-half of the increased revenue received by the school be placed in a fund to support educational innovation, and that the other half be used as teacher incentives.

The fund for educational innovation is included as an incentive to the administrators of the middle-class schools. Efforts to innovate must and should be subsidized because of the collective consumption nature which characterizes innovation. Our proposal (1) allows only school systems that have a demonstrated ability to improve students' achievement to engage in innovation. That is, if they cannot improve scores beyond the expected value, no funds will be available; (2) the benefits from the innovations will be available to society at large, and hence will not necessarily redistribute educational opportunity or income more unequally; (3) administrators who want to innovate are currently constrained by tight budgets and this would provide a resource base for experimentation.

The second half of the additional revenue would provide incentives for the teachers involved. We suggest that first-grade teachers in the school have an opportunity to compete for travel or education stipends, but no restriction need be put on the use of the funds. That is, they could be awarded as "distinguished teacher" honoraria. How many of these are awarded would depend on how significantly scores were

19. We have also developed an incentive model based on the need to motivate parents and students. See Singell and Yordon, *op. cit.*

changed, on the distribution of achievement score changes by teachers and so on. The most straightforward system would be to reward teachers directly on the basis of the score changes for which they are accountable. Hence, assuming that each teacher would have, on the average, five poverty-status students, we can summarize the range and suggested structure of the stipend as in Table 4.2.

TABLE 4.2. *Schedule of Additional Payment to Teachers*

| Composite Score in Grade Equivalent | Payment to the Teacher |
|---|---|
| .67 to .99 | no additional payment |
| 1.00 to 1.29 | $ 500 |
| 1.30 and above | $1000 |

If several teachers and school personnel are involved in such a way that the contribution of each cannot be measured, a group-incentive scheme might be necessary.

It should be stressed here that the more these incentives are based on success in a competitive structure and the less they are based on a superior's evaluation, the more efficient the incentive system will be. Hence, whenever possible, competitive systems should be created in which agreed-upon objective measures of performance are relied upon.

### The Management of the Total Program

This incentive experiment has been based on the expected total gain in tax revenue from an extra year of education at the elementary level which was estimated at $480. If achievement scores were improved by a full grade level $400 per pupil would be paid to the school and the remaining $80 per student would be required for the administration of the program. Thus, the minimum cost of this program for 1,000 students is $80,000. A rough line item breakdown of this administrative budget is given in Table 4.3.[20]

20. Cost estimates are in 1969 prices.

TABLE 4.3. *Line Budget for Administration of Program*

| Item | Cost |
|------|------|
| Transportation (Estimated at $20 per Pupil) | $20,000 |
| Administration, Including Secretarial and Clerical Work (Estimated at $15 per Pupil) | 15,000 |
| Testing and Evaluation (Estimated at $45 per Pupil) | 45,000 |
| Total | $80,000 |

The most vital aspect of this project will be structuring it such that insight with regard to the educational process can be gleaned from it. In this regard the testing and evaluation budget should probably be larger than what is suggested here. We want to stress that care must be taken to provide for adequate evaluation. Both testing and evaluation should be provided by outside independent agencies. It is our conviction that our program, if attempted on a systematic basis, may not only provide significant insights but also increase the achievement levels of poverty-status students. In addition, from the point of view of tax dollars, it may very well more than pay for itself.

The fundamental strength of the program is that its costs depend on the extent to which it is effective. Thus, if achievement scores do not change, the testing and evaluation may provide considerable insight into the educational process, but tax payers will not be asked to support another costly program where improvements did not occur.

If the program were completely successful in the sense that achievement scores were increased by a complete grade level, the total cost would be $480,000. We suggest that federal and state-local shares in the program be at the ratio of three to one, in accordance with their expected tax revenue gains (see above). Thus, the commitment on the part of the federal government would be $360,000, and the state and local governments involved should budget $120,000 for the program. How much they would actually pay would depend on the program's success. This one case in which governments may wish a program to be costly.

David K. Cohen *is professor of education at Harvard University, executive director of its Center for Educational Policy Research, and co-chairman of the Center for Law and Education. He holds the B.A. in political science from Alfred University, and the Ph.D. in social theory and intellectual history from the University of Rochester. Dr. Cohen has taught at Case-Western Reserve University and has served as director of the Race and Education Project of the U.S. Commission on Civil Rights. His current work lies in the politics of education and in school reform.*

Walter J. McCann, Jr. *is associate professor of education at Harvard University and chairman of the Administrative Career Program in the Graduate School of Education. He holds the B.A., with honors, from Wesleyan University and the J.D. in law from Harvard. He has been involved extensively in the Elementary and Secondary Education Act, the Higher Education Act, Vocational Education Act, and similar legislation. At Harvard, he has been closely connected with the Office of Economic Opportunity's Tuition Voucher Project, and with research on the relation of legal process to universities. Dr. McCann is a member of the bar in Massachusetts and the District of Columbia.*

Jerome T. Murphy *is currently completing his doctorate at the Harvard Graduate School of Education, where he is an associate in education. Columbia University granted him the B.A. and the M.A., and he also attended Georgetown Law School. He has been a math teacher, a legislative assistant in the U.S. Office of Education, assistant to the Assistant Secretary for Legislation, Department of Health, Education, and Welfare, and associate staff director of the National Advisory Council on the Education of Disadvantaged Children.*

Tyll Van Geel *is currently completing his doctorate in the Administrative Careers Program at Harvard Graduate School of Education, where he serves as assistant to Walter J. McCann. His B.A. in history comes from Princeton, and he has a J.D. from Northwestern University School of Law. Dr. Van Geel came to Harvard after serving as an attorney for the Civil Aeronautics Board in Washington, D.C.*

# 5

# Revenue-Sharing As An Incentive Device

DAVID K. COHEN, WALTER J.
McCANN, JR., JEROME T. MURPHY,
AND TYLL VAN GEEL

Dissatisfaction with the effectiveness of government in America has been growing for more than a decade. Indeed, it is probably fair to say that the problem of bureaucracy has attained the character of a national obsession. "Government" has become virtually a synonym for organizational paralysis, and it calls to mind principally the federal executive branch.

Although the reasons offered for this problem are almost as numerous as the analysts who offer them, there has been growing agreement on the remedy—decentralization. A decade ago liberals would have dismissed this as either Republican ideology or thinly disguised states'-rights propaganda, but since then the climate has changed decisively. There is growing agreement that the chief remedy for governmental ineffectiveness and inefficiency is to diminish federal power. By so doing, it is thought, states and localities will gain greater strength, vitality, and effectiveness.

One proposal for how this might be accomplished is to turn federal revenues over to state and local governments. The money would be used at the discretion of those governments, rather than being used in narrowly defined federal categorical programs. Revenue-sharing and block grants, then, have become the vehicle for decentralization within the federal system and enthusiasm for the idea has grown rapidly.

Whatever else one might say about all this, there can be no question that the proposed changes are uncommonly important. Revenue-sharing or block grants would almost surely shift the balance of power within the federal system, and they might sharply alter the role of the national government. Are these changes desirable?

Oddly enough, most of the discussion on this point has varied between minute fiscal analysis and high-flown political rhetoric. While they provide an interesting aesthetic contrast, a great gap remains between them. As nearly as we can tell, no one has explored the important issues which occupy this ground. Would unrestricted aid produce new strength at the state and local level, or only new weakness at the federal level? Is the weakness of state government the result of federal encroachment, or of local power?[1]

In this report we focus on one element of government—education. We try to determine if the political assumptions underlying the arguments for non-categorical school aid are correct.

In a situation of this sort, the choice of facts is crucial—the process of selection could irreparably bias the results. It seemed wisest, therefore, to center our analysis on a large federal education program which had stringent requirements. The reason for examining a federal program—as opposed to generally reviewing state-federal-local relations—was that such a program would most clearly reveal the role and influence of Washington agencies. That is, it would be most likely to reveal the shape of the future. We decided to review a relatively recent program for roughly the same reason. Older programs might not clearly represent the emerging trends in inter-governmental relations.

The best example, we concluded, was Title I of the 1965 Elementary and Secondary Education Act (ESEA). It is a categorical program. It is the boldest federal thrust in education thus far. Without any doubt it represents an effort to impose federal priorities on state and local school systems. If actual or potential imbalances exist in the federal system, they would surely show up in high relief here.

1. *The President's Message on Revenue Sharing* (August 1969) makes this point its chief focus.

## The Title I Program

PROGRAM AIMS

The Preamble to Title I provides:

> In recognition of the special educational needs of the children
> of low-income families and the impact that concentrations of low-
> income families have on the ability of local educational agencies
> to support adequate educational programs, the Congress hereby
> declares it to be the policy of the United States to provide financial
> assistance (as set forth in this part) to local educational agencies
> serving areas with concentrations of children from low-income
> families to expand and improve their educational programs by vari-
> ous means (including pre-school programs) which contribute par-
> ticularly to meeting the special educational needs of educationally
> deprived children.

Title I, then, is intended to serve a number of goals. It seeks
to ease the financial burden on local educational agencies arising from concentrations of low-income families, and to improve
state and local efforts to meet the educational needs of deprived
children. But while the preamble speaks largely in terms of
such educational resources as money and curriculum, the purpose of the Title is broader. If the preamble is read in conjunction with other sections, it becomes clear that the program
is designed not merely to improve program quality, but to
improve educational achievement.[2] And improving educational achievement is not an end in itself. Title I has broader
social purposes, like eliminating poverty and offering deprived
children a chance for more jobs and income.

With this scope, however, come possibilities for conflict.
Title I seeks to improve education for disadvantaged children
by providing funds with which to improve the quality of their
education. But the money is allocated to state and local school
systems, which have other problems. They may, for example,
be mainly interested in lightening their fiscal burden. The
staff and parents of target schools, on the other hand, may
understandably be more concerned with improving children's
performance. Office of Education (USOE) officials, of course,

---

2. 20 U.S.C. 241 (e) (a) (6) and (7) (1965).

would be more likely to concentrate their attention on the second of these problems.

Title I, then, contains the potential for fundamental conflict over priorities. The provisions in the act for distributing program moneys and determining how well they have been used only sharpen this problem.

ADMINISTRATIVE PROVISIONS

The central administrative mechanism of the act is the formula which determines entitlements to funds.[3] This is based on the relative incidence of poverty, as measured by income and welfare case-load. This "earmarked" money is turned over to those states which have contracted to join the program, by giving assurances that they will comply with the act. These states in turn hand the money over to the local educational agencies (LEA), once they submit detailed proposals. The state must approve these proposals, in accordance with "basic criteria" set by the USOE. These criteria concern how the money will be used and how the projects will be evaluated.

Thus, while the distribution mechanism provides a virtual entitlement for states and localities, other provisions empower the USOE to monitor, evaluate, plan, and program so as to assure that the state and local programs satisfy federal priorities. One part of the act encourages states and localities to treat the moneys as their own (in effect, as general aid), but other parts encourage federal machinery to assure that state and local operations satisfy federal criteria.

Obviously, the basic administrative provisions of Title I do nothing to relieve the potential conflict between the educational needs of poor children (or their federal advocates) and the fiscal and administrative needs of poor districts. Indeed, they only intensify it. The ultimate instrument of federal power is withholding funds. But the possibility that either the USOE or a state agency would take this step is rather remote. The entitlements built into Title I are a powerful force against it. Even if this were not the case, however, such actions are unwelcome on Capitol Hill.

3. *Ibid.*

How, then, could it be assured that the act's purposes will be met?

The answer is self-policing. Each local district is expected to evaluate its own projects, using a portion of its Title I allocation. The outcome is a local evaluation report in which the district measures its own effectiveness in reaching the goals it sets. Presumably, this report identifies local problems so that local officials or citizens could take action, and it provides information which might be of some use to the USOE and the states in re-funding decisions or in changing the basic operating criteria. The states oversee this evaluation, and the USOE oversees the states. In addition to these mandated reports, the Department of Health, Education and Welfare, OE, the National Advisory Council on the Education of Disadvantaged Children, and the states are expected to carry out other evaluations.[4]

The most conspicuous merit for this scheme was that it provided a compromise between those who wanted the federal government to offer general education aid to states and localities, and those who wanted it to play a more active reforming role.[5] Some review and control power is granted to USOE, more is granted to the states, but the act places the main reliance on self-policing by the LEA's.

Title I, then, did not cut new ground in inter-governmental relations. In every important respect the balance of power envisaged in the act reflects the clear primacy of states and localities. If the 1965 ESEA had the potential for greater centralization of the nation's school system, it lay in the discretion granted the U.S. Commissioner to develop guidelines and regulations with which to regulate program quality. The test of whether the act has in fact led to greater centralization, there-

4. 20 U.S.C. 242 (1950); 20 U.S.C. 241 (1) (1965); 20 U.S.C. 1221 (1968).
5. Three books describe the compromises that form the basis of ESEA and especially Title I. Bailey, S. and Mosher, E., *E.S.E.A.: The Office of Education Administers a Law*, Syracuse University Press, 1968; Eidenberg, E. and Morey, R., *An Act of Congress*, W. W. Norton and Company, Inc., New York, 1969; Meranto, P., *The Politics of Federal Aid to Education in 1965. A Study in Political Innovation*, Syracuse University Press, 1967.

fore, is whether its administration has permitted the imposition
of federal priorities on state and local school systems.

## Federal Administration of Title I

The USOE was not prepared for the task of administering
Title I.[6] Its staff had virtually no impact on the Title's development and would have preferred a more traditional approach
to educational aid. The agency had no experience with grants-
in-aid of the size and scope of Title I, nor had it ever been
called on to write "basic criteria" governing the approval of
projects. Herculean efforts had been made to bring in new
blood and make the agency responsive to its new responsibilities, and the agency changed significantly. New staff was
added at the top, and a total reorganization took place.

The new management partly overcame the influence of old-
line bureaucrats, but it was much more difficult to cope with
outside political pressures. These arose whenever the Office
sought to assert its authority over the program. This was best
exemplified in USOE's attempts to establish two basic
criteria—one governing the concentration of funds and the
other calling for the establishment of local community and
parent advisory councils.

FUND CONCENTRATION

USOE officials seem to have believed from the outset that
if Title I was to have any impact, the money could not be
spread thin. The original provision in the earliest draft
guidelines (Fall 1965) stated that the number of children
served could be no greater than the number of children in
the district counted under the poverty formula. This met with
strong disapproval from both the congress and professional-
interest groups, who argued that the standard was not consistent with congressional intent. Strong opposition also was
expressed about other provisions of the guidelines and regula-

6. Much of the material for this section was taken from Jerome T. Murphy,
"Federal Education Reform for the Poor: Whose Priorities Are Being Met?",
April 1970, unpulished paper.

tions. In November 1965 the word came down from Commissioner Keppel to "slenderize" the documents.[7] The concentration provision was removed. This defeat set a precedent for future efforts.

On April 14, 1967, USOE issued its first set of basic criteria, responding to what it described as a "definite need" for states to apply specific criteria in approving local projects. USOE proposed 12 criteria and included explanations of the evidence proposals should contain to show that they meet each criterion.[8] The criterion regarding concentration simply stated:

> Title I services will be programmed so that the services provided will be concentrated on a limited number of children.[9]

The supporting discussion, however, established a more precise standard.

> The investment per child on an annual basis for a program of compensatory edcational services which supplement the child's regular activities should be expected to equal about one-half the expenditure per child from state and local funds for the applicant's regular school program.[10]

Under congressional pressure, the USOE issued a "clarifying" memorandum ten days later that retreated from the thrust of the original memorandum. The new concentration standard provided only "guidance" and was not "fully applicable to every project application."[11] Thus the new standard had been rendered impotent.

USOE, of course, was not satisfied that funds were being adequately concentrated. Another memorandum was issued on November 20, 1968. The draft that went to Commissioner

7. Interview with John F. Hughes, former Director of the Division of Compensatory Education, USOE. He argues that Commissioner Keppel was under political pressure to cut back on the guidelines.

8. Memorandum from John F. Hughes, Director, Division of Compensatory Education, to chief state school officers, dated April 14, 1967, p. 1.

9. *Ibid.*, p. 4.

10. *Ibid.*, p. 4.

11. Memorandum from John F. Hughes to chief state school officers, dated April 24, 1967, p. 1.

Howe's desk for signature specifically called for implementation of the original concentration standard by 1970. At the last minute, under political pressure, the draft was pulled back by the USOE Bureau of Elementary and Secondary Education and revised.[12] The concentration standard was replaced by the hastily drawn statement:

> Plan the program so that by 1970 the average Title I expenditure per child in high-priority areas *is raised to a significant level.*[13] (Emphasis added.)

Thus, a memorandum which had begun in the Division of Compensatory Education as an attempt to accomplish greater concentration of resources emerged with no standard, even as "guidance."

ADVISORY COUNCILS

A similar pattern emerged in federal efforts to require Title I local advisory councils.

The first set of basic criteria was issued in 1967; it called for "appropriate" parent participation in Title I programs.[14] The second set of basic criteria (issued on March 18, 1968) went a step further. It called for the involvement of parents

in the early stages of program planning and in discussion concerning the needs of children in the various eligible attendance areas.[15]

Four months later (July 2, 1968), the USOE issued a separate memorandum, calling for the establishment of formal mechanism for parent involvement.[16]

This aroused considerable concern. It was one thing to discuss parent involvement, but quite another to call for formal committees which could be identified, counted, and perhaps exert some influence on the program.

12. Conversation with John F. Hughes.
13. Memorandum from Commissioner Harold Howe II to chief state school officers, dated November 20, 1968, p. 2.

14. Memorandum of April 14, 1967, *op. cit.*, p. 7.
15. Memorandum from Commissioner Harold Howe II to chief state school officers, dated March 18, 1968, p. 4.

16. Memorandum from Commissioner Harold Howe II to chief state school officers, dated July 2, 1968, p. 1.

Many educators viewed these committees as a threat to professional control, and pressure from interest groups, local educators, and the congress mounted. In less than three weeks a clarifying memorandum was sent to the chief state school officers. It retreated from the previous position, and in effect, the states were told to do as they pleased.[17]

Federal officials, naturally, remained unhappy. In 1969 the Division of Compensatory Education (DCE), not without opposition in USOE, convinced the administration to recommend that local advisory committees should be required by law. The provision was added by the House Committee on Education and Labor. It was dropped, however, during floor debate by the House of Representatives on the 1969 ESEA amendments because of strong opposition, particularly from Southern congressmen. The act which emerged from the congress was unclear on the point. More than six months after passage of the act, USOE was still engaged in a battle with education associations over USOE's authority to require councils.

A new ingredient was added in the summer of 1969, however, when it became clear that an exposé of Title I would soon be released. This study by Ruby Martin and Phyllis McClure (two former HEW employees) focused on state- and local-level failures in the administration of Title I. The study was sponsored by the NAACP Legal Defense and Education Fund and the Washington Research Project of Clark College.[18] Among other things, it resulted in a rather stringent memorandum (July 31, 1969) to chief state school officers:

> Your agency should insist on compliance with the criteria and should not hesitate to reject a project that fails to meet the criteria. . . . *Each state educational agency should adopt a plan and schedule visits for monitoring local Title I programs.* In checking on local program operations the state educational agencies should

17. Memorandum from Commissioner Harold Howe II to chief state school officers, dated July 19, 1968, p. 1.

18. *Title I of ESEA: Is It Helping Poor Children?* A report by the Washington Research Project of the Southern Center for Studies in Public Policy and the NAACP Legal Defense and Educational Fund, Inc., 1969.

take appropriate action if there is any evidence indicating violations
. . .[19] (Emphasis added.)

It is worth noting that a memorandum issued more than four
years after the law's passage asks the state to "adopt" a plan
for monitoring Title I.

At first it looked as though the balance of political power
on Title I was temporarily altered by the Martin-McClure
study. Federal officials asserted greater influence by issuing
new requirements for states and localities. In fact, on February
26, 1970, USOE revived and strengthened a long-ignored regulation requiring comparability in state and local expenditures
between Title I and non-Title I schools.[20]

Shortly after the regulation became public, however, congressional opposition developed on the grounds that it was
confusing, unworkable, and would lead to federal interference
in local school policy. The House-Senate Conference Committee, which was considering the 1969-70 amendments to ESEA,
suspended the comparability requirement for several years.
In effect, congress granted states and localities at least a temporary reprieve from executive branch enforcement activities.
In addition, the committee so defined comparability as to seriously weaken and perhaps entirely emasculate the requirement. The committee rejected the view that resources or total
instructional outlays should be comparable between Title I
and other schools in any jurisdiction. At the urging of various
professional groups they instead held that there should be
quality *apart from differences due to teachers' experience or
length of service*. Teachers' salaries, of course, comprise about
70 or 80 percent of instructional outlays, and within any district
the variation in these salaries is a strong and direct function
of experience and length of service.

Thus, to specifically exempt teacher experience and length
of service from the comparability requirement is to render

19. Memorandum from Leon M. Lessinger, Associate Commissioner for
Elementary and Secondary Education, to chief state school officers, dated
July 31, 1969.
20. Memorandum from Commissioner James E. Allen, Jr. to chief state
school officers, dated February 26, 1970.

the requirement largely ineffective. Although the revised requirement will reach gross cores of discrimination and negligence, it will not affect the structural causes of inequality among rich and poor schools within districts.

This episode nicely illustrates the context in which USOE officials operate. Most federal legislators are sure to be more responsive to the wishes of state and local school officials than to bureaucrats in the executive branch. This is especially true if there are no contrary pressures on state and local school authorities or congressmen from the program's clients. In this situation, the sole constituency of the Title I administrators is the congress and the state and local school system, not the poor people whose children the legislation is supposed to assist. Lacking counter-pressures, federal officials are relatively powerless to impose standards on state and local school systems.

These constraints permeate the operation of the program. Their effect can be observed both in the behavior and attitudes of the Title I staff, and in federal program-monitoring activities.

THE TITLE I STAFF

To understand the problems of administering Title I, one must begin with the simple fact that OE simply has not had the staff required to operate the program. The Title I staff is divided into two branches—operations and program development. As recently as January 1970, those two branches employed 14 professionals.[21]

This meant, for example, that all monitoring was handled by three "area-desk" officers; the area-desk man who dealt with Massachusetts, for example, had responsibility for 23 other states, Puerto Rico and the Virgin Islands.[22] In addition, he spent most of his time on other projects, which had practically nothing to do with Title I. He had no assistants and

21. In the early days of the program, the Division of Program Operations (later the Division of Compensatory Education) approached its authorized personnel strength of 82 (including professional and clerical staff) but subsequently dwindled (Bailey and Mosher, *op. cit.*, p. 93).

22. Interview with Benjamin Rice, Midwest and Eastern Regional Representative, Division of Compensatory Education, USOE.

a substantial part of his Title I work involved drafting replies to congressional mail.

Recently Title I staff levels have been increased. But even if we assume that these increases are sufficient to allow USOE to gain more control of the Title I program (which seems dubious), that would only be possible if the agency desired such control. And this simply is not the orientation of the USOE staff.

In DCE, for example, the area-desk officers take a passive role with respect to the states. The Massachusetts desk officer described his relationship with the Massachusetts Title I director as "very nice." In the six months preceding the interview reported here, they had met once and talked occasionally on the telephone. He viewed his job as one of trouble-shooting, answering complaints, and providing services. If he found the limited staff situation frustrating, it was not because he could not monitor the states, but because he could not give them assistance.

To some extent, such an attitude reflects an accurate evaluation of the real situation which a federal official faces. With inadequate staff and little independent power, an official is unlikely to assume a vigorous monitoring role. For one thing, he is unable to deliver as an "enforcer." But if by some chance he should, he is almost sure to provoke congressional opposition to his action. Given this dilemma, a low profile is easy to understand; it means survival.

POLITICAL CONSTRAINTS

Even if the staff were increased one-hundred-fold, these external political limits would not change.

This is nicely illustrated by OE's execution of its responsibility to audit state and local programs. According to the Martin-McClure study:

> The audit reports have brought to light numerous violations of the law and have recommended that millions of dollars be recovered by the federal government. Yet in only three cases has the Office of Education sought and received restitution of funds ille-

gally spent. . . . Even in the most flagrant cases of unlawful use of the money . . . the Office of Education failed to act.[23]

The reasons for inaction are essentially political. First, in the early days of Title I there was pressure to get the program moving quickly and to get federal-state relations off on the right foot. There was a natural tendency to accentuate the positive and overlook alleged misuses. Second, there was tremendous pressure on Title I administrators to generate evidence of the program's success, so that the administration could justify the program to the public and congress. Third, there was fear that if USOE pressed its priorities the congress would replace categorical programs with general aid, in which case USOE would have even less influence. The political costs of seeking return of allegedly misused funds, for example (which the state viewed as "their" money), had to be carefully weighed. Experience suggested that there was a high probability of losing such struggles. USOE staff remembered Commissioner Keppel's abortive withdrawal of funds from Chicago for civil-rights violations,[24] and Keppel's departure soon thereafter.

Most important, federal administrators always seek to build a constituency for their program. In the case of Title I, much of their attention was focused on the congress, and state and local school administrators. There appears never to have been any thought about encouraging other, counter-constituencies. From this perspective, it would be one thing to urge a state to follow certain criteria, but an entirely different matter to accuse it of misusing funds. However much a particular congressman might criticize waste and misuse, if it occurred in his district his response would usually be different.

CONCLUSIONS

Viewed from the federal level, then, it seems that the executive branch has been unable to gain much control of the Title I program. This is due in some part to the lack of sufficient

23. Title I of ESEA . . . , *op. cit.*, p. 97.
24. Bailey and Mosher, *op. cit.*, pp. 151, 152.

staff, but mostly it arises from the strong tradition of localism in American politics generally, and education particularly. The education professions maintain effective national offices in Washington, and they are in the habit of expressing their commitment to state and local dominance forcefully and directly, to both USOE and the congress. The congress itself is deeply committed to localism in education, not only as a matter of ideology but also self-interest. Few congressmen welcome executive interference in the flow of funds to their states or districts. Finally, there is the OE staff itself, almost all of which has been recruited from the professions whose educational priorities Title I was designed to change.

## *State Administration of Title I*

As we noted earlier, the states have a central role in administering Title I: they are supposed to review and approve project applications, audit and monitor the on-going projects, and evaluate the results. With the products of these efforts, the states are then supposed to improve the program's operation, and satisfy the Office of Education that everything is in order.

Has the USOE been able to compel the states to carry out these functions to its satisfaction?

The evidence on this point is scanty and very incomplete. In general, the picture which emerges from our investigation is that state administration of Title I resembles nothing so much as its management in Washington. Typically it ranges between weakness and indifference. Most state education agencies cannot be said to have real control of the program, if by this we mean effective monitoring, evaluation, and auditing. Nonetheless, they do have political control of the programs—even state agencies which have the least administrative capacity are able to effectively resist federal priorities and pressures.

It is important to point out, however, that state administration is neither uniformly bad, not uniformly at variance with federal priorities. A few states have followed federal initiatives in a few areas, not because of irresistible federal pressure, but because of state decisions which were consistent with one or another federal priority. Perhaps the fairest characterization of the situation, then, is that the states are pretty well free to do as they like.

These conclusions are not, however, based on a multitude of careful case studies of state administration of Title I. Few such studies have been done, and those that exist are, at this writing, incomplete and unpublished. We have used them, but our main attention has been directed at understanding the situation in one state—Massachusetts.

PROGRAM MONITORING

In Massachusetts, the Title I program is administered in the Bureau of Elementary and Secondary Education.[25] The full-time staff of the Office which manages Title I includes three supervisors, a project director, two secretaries, and one auditor. This leaves six people to monitor roughly 430 projects with a total cost of $15 million.[26] At this staffing level it would be impossible to even visit each project once a year, let alone understand what they are doing.

Were there no staffing problems, however, the agency's posture would not change. The state Title I director views his job as providing technical assistance and service to local school districts. He refers to local control as *"The Battle Hymn of the Republic* of New England educators," and believes that initiative and leadership should come from the local level.

In effect, the Title I director expresses the same reluctance to interfere with local prerogatives that federal officials express about interfering with state prerogatives. Moreover, he sees his role *vis-à-vis* local districts—techinal assistance and service—the same way that his federal counterparts perceive their role toward the states. To paraphrase Daniel Elazar,[27] what usually happens is that federal, state, and local educators, working in the same program, trained in the same schools, and active in the same professional associations, think along the

25. The remainder of this sub-section taken from Murphy, *op. cit.*
26. Estimates provided by Robert L. Jeffrey, Title I Office, Massachusetts Department of Education.
27. Elazar, Daniel J., *American Federalism: A View from the States*, New York: Thomas Y. Crowell Company, 1966, p. 149.

same lines and have relatively little trouble in reaching a meeting of minds.

This is manifest in the Department's financial management activities. The second HEW audit report on Massachusetts concluded that "significant improvements in procedures and practices are needed at both the state and local levels."[28] The audit found that for each of the fiscal years 1966, 1967, and 1968 the Department allowed federal allotment of more than $1 million to lapse because of ineffective management.[29] The situation in Boston dramatizes this problem:

> Even though the amount of $263,000 was unused by the City of Boston in fiscal year 1968, we found that certain eligible attendance areas with high concentrations of children from low-income families in the City of Boston were receiving minimal services for meeting the special educational needs of these children. . . . We were advised by City of Boston program directors that the limited availability of funds precluded them from providing additional services in these areas.[30]

The reason for this is simple: state auditing activities are practically non-existent. In addition, since the only audit report that local districts are required to submit is a one-page sheet that breaks down Title I expenditures by categories, the state knows next to nothing about local practices or allocations. The state Title I director does not believe that money is being misused in Massachusetts, but admits that he has no way of proving this. He would like to have more auditors for Title I—at one time there were three—but argues that it is difficult to get competent people to work for the department.

EVALUATION

Our review of the Massachusetts Education Department's work with Title I evaluation reveals a similar style of

28. HEW Audit Agency, Report on Review of Grants Awarded to the Commonwealth of Massachusetts Under Title I, Elementary and Secondary Education Act of 1965, dated January 23, 1969, p. 3.

29. *Ibid.*, p. 4.

30. *Ibid.*, p. 20.

operation.[31] Evaluation in the state goes on at two levels. The state conducts its own survey of Title I projects, collecting data for its annual report to the USOE. At the same time, it is involved in various ways with the local districts' self-evaluation efforts.

The results of the state's own evaluation work—contained in its annual Title I report—are such that it is impossible to determine anything about the effects of particular Title I projects—or, for that matter, the entire program.

The report shows, for example, achievement test scores computed before and after Title I participation for several groups of children, by grade and test used. But it isn't clear whether the results come from two districts or 200; thus we cannot gauge the meaning of the findings. Furthermore, the data are averaged over the state rather than being presented for groups of schools or school districts. This effectively removes any chance of comparing the relative benefits of different Title I programs.

Moreover, if we look behind the report, at the data on which it is based, things do not improve. Aggregated test scores are reported to the state for entire projects. Since they are not identified with particular students, individual schools, or identifiable program activities, the scores could not be used to evaluate projects, schools, or programs. The evidence in the state report is meaningless, then, because the data it collected could serve no conceivable evaluative purpose.

The problem, however, extends a good deal beyond the evaluation forms. The schedule of evaluation reporting is not articulated with the budgeting cycle, so that budgets are decided *before* the evaluation of Title I programs is complete. Even if the evaluation report were well-conceived, it would be of little use. The same thing is true of other aspects of the state's annual report. Data on the satisfaction of program

31. The remainder of the sub-section is based in part on David K. Cohen and Tyll van Geel, "Public Education," in *The State and the Poor*, Samuel H. Beer and Richard E. Barringer, eds. (Cambridge, Mass.: Winthrop Publishers, Inc., 1970).

goals are not consistently reported by school, activity, or project. The reporting varies between the general (state-wide averages) and the particular (examples of one aspect of a single project which evaluators found particularly appealing). As a result the state lacks information with which it can conduct comparative studies of program effectiveness. There is no way of determining which approach to improving achievement or training teachers produces the biggest improvements, or the cheapest ones, or the best ones.

Of course, the state's own evaluation procedure is not the whole story. In theory at least, the state employs the results of local self-evaluation to monitor projects and up-grade the quality of programs within the state. But a review of state and local efforts in this connection suggests that after an initial effort to make use of evaluation in Boston, the Massachusetts State Education agency lapsed into an almost completely passive posture toward Title I evaluation.

THE BOSTON STORY

The first "year" of Title I operations ran from January to June, 1966. Boston's evaluation program for this period relied mainly on questionnaires sent to parents, teachers and students. That summer the State Department of Education suggested that an inter-university team "make an independent evaluation of the [Boston Title I evaluation] program," to advise Boston about modifications for the coming school year.[32] The team was given power to authorize a stoppage of Boston's Title I funds if Boston did not cooperate in the development of a better evaluation scheme.[33]

The university team met for the first time in June 1966 and called itself the Inter-University Evaluation Committee (IUEC). During that summer it assessed the Title I summer-program evaluation procedures, and gathered information

32. This section of the paper was partly based on Tyll van Geel, "Evaluation and Federalism," April 1970. Unpublished paper.

33. Inter-University Evaluation Committee, "Evaluation Report No. 1 to the Office of Program Development," August 31, 1966, p. 1.

about the regular school program and evaluation procedures. The result was a report on problems in the Boston evaluation program, and an outline for the steps required to improve it.

The IUEC recommendations contained several major components: precise definition of program objectives and the means of attainment; explicit hypotheses regarding expected results; a schedule and procedure for collecting data; the collection of similar data for control groups; and the establishment of a data bank to facilitate comparisons within and among programs.

In this instance, the state, through the IUEC, had provided as close supervision and assistance for the improvement of evaluation as could be expected. Despite this effort, nothing came of the whole endeavor.[34]

The first difficulty was evident when, in September, the IUEC and Boston Title I staff discussed the first report; IUEC reported that "Because insufficient time had elapsed between the submission of the report and the joint meeting, the response to the report was more general than it might have been. . . ."[35] Following that meeting—at which it was agreed that Boston's Title I staff would start to implement the recommendations—contacts were maintained. By early November IUEC reviewed Boston's efforts again, and "found them variously deficient although markedly improved over those of the previous year. IUEC criticized the lack of specificity in objectives, the absence of time schedules for data collection, the lack of clearly identified control groups . . ." and other things.[36] Not much progress had taken place since the first report.

In fact, there was an underlying dispute with regard to the IUEC role. IUEC saw itself as an objective outside critic which

34. *IUEC Report No. 1*, p. 19.
35. *IUEC Report No. 2*, January 15, 1967, p. 1. A major failing on the part of the IUEC was its reluctance to cut off Boston's funds. The committee members, fearing the injustice that would be done to the target children if Boston lost the Title I funds, were disinclined to exercise their prerogative. Whether deliberately or inadvertently, Boston took advantage of this reluctance.
36. *Ibid.*, pp. 2-3.

was to make recommendations that Boston would implement. Boston officials, however, regarded the IUEC as a purely advisory body, whose presence was due only to state insistence. Thus, as of the last IUEC report (August 15, 1967), 17 of the original 28 IUEC recommendations had either not been executed, or had only been considered by Boston, or had been carried out so poorly that the IUEC soundly criticized the effort. Of the 11 recommendations which had been carried out, three had been executed by the IUEC itself.[37]

The fundamental difficulty, of course, was Boston's resistance to the nature of the IUEC plan, and the assumptions about the role of evaluation which lay behind it. Boston opposed obtaining the data necessary for the execution of the evaluation design, refused to accept matching students on the basis of race, rejected the idea of making intra-program and inter-program comparisons, and resisted the establishment of an adequate student data bank. In effect, the Boston schools had no desire to make program decisions based on evaluation results, and no intention of submitting to evaluation by the state or its agents. This was well-illustrated by the gesture which led to IUEC's demise. In June of 1967 Boston requested that IUEC restrict its use of the evaluation data—apparently to preclude its public release. IUEC refused, considering such an attempt to restrain the public use of data to be counter to the whole concept of evaluation.

By August, the IUEC had disbanded. Its members had concluded that they could not compel the Boston schools to design and execute a useful evaluation of the Title I program. They were unwilling to recommend the withdrawal of Title I funds—mainly because they thought it would penalize the children more than the schools. In the absence of any such sanctions, of course, there was no incentive for Boston to be responsive. Thus the state withdrew its authority to stop the flow of funds to Boston, and things went on as they had before. Boston's evaluation report for the 1966-67 school year read as though IUEC had never existed, and this report set the

37. Based on a comparison of the two IUEC reports.

pattern for subsequent efforts.[38]

Looking back over the five years after Title I came to Boston, then, all the state's attempts to improve the quality of evaluation were simply absorbed. Boston simply did the minimum necessary to meet what it regarded as irrelevant and unpleasant requirements: it delayed execution of the state recommendations; it refused to comply with some suggestions, and executed other requests so poorly that they needed to be done all over again; it argued at great length about the inappropriateness of the test in relation to the objectives of the program, and it left the program objectives vague.

The conclusion which emerges from this dreary story is that in general, the state education agencies control the Title I program as a political but not as administrative matter. The agencies can resist federal priorities, but they either have none of their own, or they have not the will to impose them on local districts. With a few exceptions, the state agencies relate to the LEA's in the same way the Office of Education relates to the state agencies. Real initiative and power in the system rests at the bottom.

## Conclusions

This does not mean that the Title I program is a failure, or that local school districts have failed in their obligations under the act. Neither of these issues has been under discussion here. Our concern is with a different issue—what the administration of this program reveals about the balance of power within the nation's school system.

There is no evidence that federal power has grown perceptibly as a result of Title I. In addition, while the states' poor performance in managing Title I is probably due in some part to their historic pattern of resistance to federal authority, it arises chiefly from the fact that state education agencies have

38. Ohrenberger, William H., Vaughn, Mary E., Kennedy, Paul A., *Boston Public Schools, Elementary Enrichment Programs, Evaluation 1966-1967*, October 1967. (Mimeo.)

little administrative vitality. Although their constitutional and statutory powers are enormous, their relations to localities typically have been cautious, careful, and passive.

What does this imply for revenue-sharing or block grant proposals?

The most important point is that in education, at least, such proposals cannot be justified on the grounds of growing federal dominance. It is no longer sufficient to argue that block grants and revenue-sharing are politically and administratively sound because they will strengthen state and local government by reducing federal power. If state and local government need to be strengthened, it must be because they are weak, not because the federal education agency is strong. If there is a sound political and administrative rationale for non-categorical aid, it must be that it will strengthen state government, not that it will reduce federal power.

Would non-categorical aid have this effect?

The result would probably be precisely the opposite. Revenue-sharing or block grants might reduce federal power in education, but that is not the cause of the state school agencies' weakness. Furthermore, there is no reason to believe that the states' administrative capacity would increase. Those agencies have a long history of passivity in relation to the localities, and we can imagine no way in which more unrestricted money alone would change this pattern. The states' share of local revenue has grown dramatically over the last few decades, but there is no evidence that the states' power has grown as a result. Finally, there is enormous pressure on the states to provide more support for local education agencies. The combination of these factors makes it almost certain that new funds would simply be distributed, with little or no effect on the vitality or capacity of the state agency.

This might be a matter of little concern were there no need for improved performance at the state level. The conclusion which emerges from our investigation, however, is that there is a grave need for increased strength. Both state and federal school agencies have developed few of the capacities needed to carry their weight within the federal system. This is not to say that there are no good political or administrative reasons for non-categorical aid. Quite the contrary, it is a perfectly appropriate response to unnecessary constraints on otherwise capable, energetic, and responsive government agencies. It just happens, however, that this is not the problem with state management of education in America. The difficulty is the lack of capacity, the absence of energy and an inability to respond to much besides the political dominance of local school systems.

WHAT, THEN, IS THE ANSWER?

The weaknesses in the federal system must be recognized for what they are. The problem is not that state government has grown weak as a result of federal encroachment, but that at both levels the development of governmental capacity has not kept pace, either with the society's economic and social development, with the growth of educational institutions, or with the population's demand for improved services. Thus, if our concern is retaining a proper balance within the federal system, our aim must be to increase capacity at both of these levels of government. In public education, at least, the danger is not that localities will be stripped of their rightful prerogatives and responsibilities, but that the states and the federal government will not gain capacity to carry their unique share—that is, to identify and respond effectively to state-wide or national issues. Revenue-sharing or block grants would probably weaken the ability of the USOE in this regard, without strengthening the states.

Seymour S. Bellin *is associate professor (sociology) in the Department of Psychiatry of Tufts University School of Medicine. He attended Brooklyn College, where he earned the B.A. in economics, the Sorbonne, from which he received a certificate, and Columbia University, where he was awarded the M.A. in economics and the Ph.D. in sociology. Dr. Bellin has conducted research on various public policies and programs in the domains of health, education, and welfare. Most recently, these studies have included a national study of citizen participation, and an evaluation of new forms of health care. In addition to his duties at the School of Medicine, Dr. Bellin teaches in the department of sociology at Tufts.*

Shirley S. Bellin *is a clinical psychologist with a specialty in learning disorders and child therapy. She holds the B.A. in psychology from the New School for Social Research, the M.S. in clinical and school psychology from the City College of New York, and is currently a candidate for the Ph.D. in psychology at Syracuse University. Mrs. Bellin has done research in mental retardation, and formerly worked as supervisor of psychological interns at Syracuse State School. She is also a New York State certified school psychologist.*

# 6

# Teacher Incentives Tied to Pupil Performance

SEYMOUR S. BELLIN AND
SHIRLEY S. BELLIN

## Introduction

Despite our large national investment of resources and man-power in education, a crescendo of discontent has risen about the proportion of children who fail to reach their academic and intellectual potential. In addition, there has been a tax-payers' revolt precipitated, on one hand, by local fiscal crises and, on the other hand, by the perpetual demand for additional funds for education.

The schools have not ignored this situation. Indeed, the history of education is one of numerous innovations, a continuous search for the ultimate panacea. There are some bold and dramatic experiments, however, that, even after a half a century, have remained isolated and are periodically "redis-covered." For the most part, they have had minimal impact on the fundamental premises and structure of our educational institutions. [25]

It is against this background that the burgeoning demand for public accountability must be understood. [3, 4, 19, 21] There always has been a commitment to accountability, but historically it has been primarily directed towards inputs (resources) rather than towards outcomes in terms of pupil learning. In the absence of a uniform and systematic audit (especially of outcomes), there has been no way of evaluating the extent to which educational goals are being met and the relative effectiveness of various innovations in organizing the educational process. The development of educational audits to complement the traditional administrative audit would constitute a major step forward in achieving accountability. Clearly, they would introduce a way to justify the request for additional funds, new programs, or other innovations. By themselves, however, they would not necessarily assure sufficient impetus for change.

During the past several years, public attention has been drawn to performance-contracting in education. [1, 9, 20] Incentive pay for teachers tied to pupil performance has been examined as one way of achieving accountability in terms of educational achievement. Whereas the audit provides the gauge of performance, the financial incentive provides the impetus to take the results of it seriously. This paper attempts to examine the philosophic, technical, and political issues involved in such an incentive scheme and to appraise it as an instrument of public policy. [6]

## *Incentive Pay Tied to Pupil Performance:*
## *What It Is and How It Is Supposed To Work*

The concept of payment contingent upon results is not novel. It received new impetus a few years ago, however, when several schools contracted with private educational firms in which payment was based on the achievement of specified objectives. Recently, the Office of Economic Opportunity mounted a large-scale demonstration project to evaluate the effectiveness of such performance-contracting. With few exceptions, this effort involved private educational firms to work with selected pupils manifesting severe educational deficits, usually in reading or in mathematics. (More recently, one local public-school system turned over an entire elementary school to a private educational firm on a performance-contract basis.)

Performance-contracting outside the regular school system has been justified by the distinction between the "politics of innovation" and the "politics of adoption." [1] Experimental innovation often can be more readily undertaken *outside* the school system because independent agencies presumably are freer of administrative, legal, and political constraints. Once the practical utility of an innovation has been demonstrated, it can be turned over to a regular school, which must then face the issues involved in facilitating adoption and implementation. In principle, the use of outside firms in a two-stage process of innovation can be useful, although two caveats must be mentioned. First, there is a risk that, either for reasons of self-interest or ideological perspective, outside private firms, particularly if they are commercial, will favor innovations in educational technology which enhance their own advantage (*e.g.*, possible sales of teaching machines or curriculum materials) rather than in organization, manpower, and approach. A second, and perhaps more important, consideration is the risk that extramural contracting can become an institutionalized "cop-out" which makes it possible for public schools to escape their own responsibility for unsatisfactory pupil performance.

Performance-contracting with outside firms, however, constitutes a challenge which schools, both public and private, cannot ignore for long. *If, indeed, such firms can successfully guarantee educational results, then the public school system will experience enormous political pressure to explain why it cannot do likewise.* Assuming that performance-contracting proves successful, the next logical step is to extend the concept to the public school itself. One form involves rewarding teachers for improved pupil achievement, usually referred to as incentive pay.

Incentive pay, supplementing the basic salary schedule, is a form of merit pay. [34, 10] It differs however, from the prevailing merit pay plans which typically are based upon one of three sets of criteria: the acquisition of special qualifications (*i.e.*, credentials attesting to formal training or experience), rating of teacher classroom performance, or the scope of job responsibility. Incentive-pay-tied-to-pupil-outcomes is free from gratuitous assumptions about effectiveness of prevailing teaching methods implicit in these other schemes. It substitutes, instead, a pragmatic principle as a basis for merit pay: it rewards that which works. A premium is placed upon the adoption of an open and innovative approach to students and education, and upon greater individual attention to each pupil.

It is important that performance-contracting be proposed as bonus rather than base pay because there is no ostensible risk or penalty associated with non-cooperation or failure. It may be seen as both an inducement to accept the principle of an educational audit as well as a means of focusing attention upon results.

This form of merit pay offers decided advantages over promotion and dismissal as an incentive device. Promotions are not only limited in number, but remove good teachers from the very thing which they do well: classroom teaching. Dismissals, on the other hand, are relatively rare because of tenure rules and contracts which are backed by relatively strong professional organizations. In practice, dismissal defines minimal standards of competence and morality, thereby excluding teachers whose competence is marginal. By contrast with promotion or dismissal, merit pay affords a graduated reward in proportion to results produced which, in principle, is available to *all* teachers.

Bonus pay also may minimize the loss of some experienced and superior teachers who presently may seek more attractive financial opportunities elsewhere. Moreover, it may draw more talented people into teaching.

Ultimately, the same principle of accountability, applied to the process of teacher selection and training, may bring to the schools a cadre of individuals who are more compatible with the new directions in education. The critical question remains, however, whether a teacher-incentive plan can accomplish substantial gains on the basis of the *present* teacher manpower pool. There are those who believe that the solution to our educational ills lies primarily in better selection and training, implicitly assuming that teachers are unchangeable and that teaching, performance is best explained by personality characteristics which are minimally influenced by environmental constraints. A contrary view, however, prevails in the social sciences. Human socialization is seen as a continuous process throughout the life cycle and human behavior is interpreted as a function of the interplay between changing dispositional and environmental characteristics. This is consistent with developments in organizational science which suggest that an organization may exhibit differences in morale and productivity despite a relatively stable personnel composition.

Some of the strength of incentive pay as an instrument of public policy is in its political and administrative advantages over alternative mechanisms for achieving better educational results. This pay is positive and permissive rather than punitive: while it imposes constraints in terms of curriculum and periodic testing, it requires a minimum of direct day-to-day operational intervention into local school activities. It leaves open the issue of the content and methods and, hence, intrudes relatively little upon professional prerogatives. Furthermore, it does not alter the present structure of governance or accountability—the balance between teachers, administrators, the public constituency at large, or its representatives who make up the school committees. Therefore, such a plan is compatible with American political tradition which favors decentralization and home rule.

## Critics and Critiques

Incentive plans appear disarmingly simple and straightforward, yet they have generated sharp controversy. Although the most vigorous opposition has been led by the two national teachers' organizations, it is by no means confined to them. Some administrators, educators, scholars, and parents have voiced grave concerns about incentive plans. [16] Despite the fact that a few schools scattered around the country have already undertaken to experiment with performance-contracting, the dominant mood of most schools appears to

be one of skepticism and caution. This mood has been reinforced during the past year by preliminary negative conclusions reported in the press on the large-scale demonstration
conducted by OEO in performance-contracting. This paper
attempts a systematic review of the concerns that have been
or are likely to be expressed by various participants in the
educational process in order to identify issues that may affect
the adoption of the scheme.

In the ensuing discussion, these issues have been organized
in terms of their implications for the chief participants in the
educational enterprise: the pupils, the teachers, the administrators, and the citizen governing bodies. An examination of
these issues reveals that they can be attributed to two components: (1) the very concept of an incentive itself; and (2) the
educational audit which is integral to such a plan.

THE IMPLICATIONS FOR PUPILS

An important theme in the public discussions of performance-
contracting is its implications for pupils, the ultimate justifica-
tion of the educational venture. Two related questions are
raised: (1) will an incentive scheme work in achieving the
main intended effect—raising academic performance?; and (2)
are there (unintended) "side effects" which offset whatever
gains may be achieved?

*Will It Work? The Main Intended Effects.* There appears
to be a general skepticism among teachers that an incentive
scheme tied to results will be successful. There is fatalism
that not much can be done, at least within the setting of the
school, about under-achieving pupils from poverty and minority populations, despite teachers' best efforts and training. The
findings reported by the Coleman study and evaluations of
compensatory education and "Head Start" programs have reinforced the conviction that the die is cast even before the child
enters school. [7, 12] Initially, this fatalistic mood was chal-
lenged by the willingness of private educational firms to gam-
ble their profits upon success. Recently, however, preliminary
conclusions, reported in the press about the outcome of the
large-scale experiment in extramural performance-contracting

undertaken last year by the Federal Office of Economic Opportunity, have been discouraging. Although the final judgment on this experiment is not yet in, there are good reasons why such an extramural program is likely to realize limited gains and why such results should not be generalized to proposals for *intramural* performance contracting. At the same time, there are lessons to be learned from the external demonstration in designing an internal incentive scheme.

It is essential to keep in mind that a *process*—not a simplistic or mechanical "input-output" model—is involved. This statement implies not only a complex system of influences and interactions, but also one in which long-term effects may be more significant than short-term (thus, possibly unmeasurable) effects. [26]

Seymour Gang, former principal of Harlem P.S. 92, reported the importance of intervening early, involving the total faculty, and maintaining a continuous program. [8] Of greater significance was the total community involvement which brought about positive and durable social-psychological changes which had an appreciable impact on school-community relations. While it is difficult to establish cause and effect connections, it is more important to establish the interactive and field-wide nature of the forces affecting student involvement and achievement. Any single element of a system, therefore, must be assessed in context.

In this connection, one may appreciate the limitations of extramural programming insofar as it ignores the essential function of the educational environment as a system. Moreover, the "compensatory" concept, in addition to treating the child in a segmented way, assumes a "blaming the victim" posture rather than an interactional hypothesis. [29]

Even if the results of performance-contracting with private firms prove successful, however, teachers are likely to remain somewhat skeptical for still another reason. Some teachers maintain that their past efforts to innovate have been thwarted by the lack of resources and of discretionary authority over conditions that affect pupil motivation and learning. Furthermore, even when resources have been available, innovation has not been supported and has even been actively discouraged by administrators and/or the school governing committee. [5, 14, 33] There seems to be no apparent reason why things should change with the introduction of incentive pay for teachers.

Teachers recognize that they have limited power and influence in the bureaucratic structure of the school. Basic policy and, frequently, actual curriculum are beyond their domain. Moreover, they argue that the school itself is a relatively circumscribed system within a broader environment, that of a cultural-political structure, which pervades the children's lives and the lives of their families, a primary socializing influence on the motivational and intellectual functioning of the child. It is little wonder that the teacher feels justified in rejecting the heavy burden of primary-change agent imposed upon him by a program which may charge him with more than his actual share of responsibility and power. He can view such a program only as unrealistic and unjust.

*Is the Cure Worse than the Disease? Side-Effects.* Concern has been expressed about the implications of an incentive system and the educational audit which is essential to it for the academic and non-academic well-being of the pupil. These include apprehensions about the narrowing of education, the substitution of extrinsic rather than intrinsic motivations in education for pupils, and possible psychological consequences that might ensue from the choice of educational goals and the testing process itself. These potential risks are accentuated insofar as teachers might be motivated to subvert the intent of the testing program.

A major theme in the growing debate on accountability involves the apparent conflict between two broad educational objectives: "managerial" goals—emphasizing cognitive and technical skills oriented to instrumental or practical ends, and humanistic goals—stressing the values of personal development and democratic citizenship. The philosophy, methods, and anticipated consequences of accountability (with its implied notions of a clearly defined product, standardized curricula, and rigorous measurement) are alleged to be in fundamental contradiction to the goals of humanistic education.

While it is important to respect the broader (humanistic) objectives, it seems neither necessary nor desirable that the more limited (and traditional) skills be ignored. Placed within a framework of a developmental learning sequence, both reading and mathematics, particularly in the elementary grades, constitute a legitimate focus for achievement. It is not intended to suggest that these preclude other areas of concern. They can, however, in the case of low-income and minority groups, become a progressive educational handicap and, therefore, merit special consideration. It is an equally important factor that they, in particular, are presently amenable to more satisfactorily standardized measurement than other subject areas. Although other educational goals are not as well-defined and operationalized at this time, there is no intrinsic reason why, in time, satisfactory operational measures could not be developed. At the present time, however, on the basis of practicality as well as their own essential value, reading and mathematics skills lend themselves to early explorations in accountability programs. [13, 15]

This is a source of consternation to those who fear the potential and unintended narrowing effects of just such programmatic emphases. Evidence suggests, however, that increased competence in these very skills actually enhances other areas of learning.

Additional reservations have been raised about the testing and evaluation process itself which is integral to any incentive scheme. Most salient, perhaps, is the fear that tests will tend in various ways to narrow the breadth of educational goals. First, there may be a tendency to "teach to the test," since coaching pupils to test items might be difficult to resist. Furthermore, the very process of evaluation itself will deflect time and attention away from teaching and learning. Moreover, some educators fear that it might lead pupils to place undue value upon test scores rather than upon the subject-matter itself. This might also have the effect of intensifying competition among pupils, thus distorting their interpersonal relationships, or generating excssive personal anxiety.

Safeguards against the risks of narrowing effects of an incentive scheme or the negative side-effects of the testing process can be devised in the form of periodic sampling of pupil performance in other subject-matter areas, as well as personal and social adjustment (through systematic observation and interviewing as well as standardized tests). In the final analysis, however, the impact of such a program upon the pupils depends a great deal upon the attitudes of the faculty and administration toward it, how its results are used, and how it is monitored. An effort should be made to rationalize the evaluation activities so that they are integrated into the educational process. [32]

Another issue frequently raised in conjunction with routinized testing involves the alleged constraints it imposes upon the discretion of local schools and teachers to innovate and to tailor educational content and techniques to the needs and style of their pupils. Teachers, in particular, view periodic educational audits as a further erosion of their professional discretion which, they feel, already is extremely limited. They fear being caught in a double bind in which they will be more rigorously held accountable for results at a time when they have diminishing control over many of the critical conditions which influence effective learning. One solution that needs consideration, of course, is enfranchising teachers with relevant and necessary discretionary authority while, at the same time, assuring effective accountability in terms of pupil educational outcomes.

Some measure of constraint in the form of a standardized curriculum content (and tests) is inevitable; it is a necessary condition to a system of accountability as well as a response to demands and pressures of a highly mobile society at large. The belief that universal quality education can be delivered in a more economic and efficient manner without a method of measuring results, or that the present lack of such accountability can continue in education, is politically naive, and both empirically as well as philosophically unjustified. Much that has passed for educational practice has been, in reality, poor education at best. Such widespread educational delinquency can be perpetuated only in the continuing absence of education audit.

TEACHERS, ADMINISTRATORS, AND LAYMEN

The efficacy of an incentive scheme which singles out teachers, and the possible negative academic and non-academic side effects of such a plan are concerns shared by many teachers, administrators and laymen. There are, in addition, special reservations characteristically raised by each of these participants which will be considered below. In addition to their actual merit, these issues have a considerable bearing on the political feasibility of an incentive scheme as a strategy for system-wide change.

*Issues Pertinent to Teachers and Their Organizations: The View From the Line.* Since the proposed incentive plan most directly involved teachers, their apprehensions demand serious attention. Official and unofficial views expressed by representatives of teachers' organizations and by rank-and-file teachers reflect considerable resistance to intrmural performance-contracting. [16] Despite some softening of this stance (reflected in the scattered schools which are experimenting with some form of teacher performance-contracting), opposition remains widespread. In addition to the more general misgivings described earlier which they share, there are a few special themes evident in comments on performance-contracting plans.

*Individual and Collective Security.* One worry is that inequities in the opportunity to earn merit pay and the possible invidious meanings given to differential earnings may cause dissension and poor morale among teachers. The prospects for assuring equal opportunity for merit pay for *all* teachers is far from a self-evident conclusion: actual experience with performance-contracting within schools is limited. If opportunity for incentive pay is restricted to a few teachers, there may be envy and resentment even if the lucky few are chosen in a fair manner. Furthermore, an individual incentive scheme may present special problems in those primary schools which have instituted team-teaching or a departmental system in which there is specialization by subject matter. (Some primary schools have introduced this feature as early as the fourth grade.) Thus, antagonism may be felt by teachers whose particular subject matter areas are excluded from incentive pay, especially if they feel that they contribute significantly, though indirectly, to pupil achievement in the target subject areas. Differential earnings among teachers also might lead to invidious judgments and to a preoccupation with equality in pupil assignment. The net consequence, it is feared, would be to undermine teacher cooperation in the service of both better teaching and collective self-interest.

Incentive pay plans based on pupil performance (like piece-rate or bonus plans in industry) jeopardize the principle of collective action. Teachers who earn (or hope to earn) substantial bonuses on the basis of individual incentives are likely to have a diluted commitment to the fate of their colleagues and their organizations.

Furthermore, there is the suspicion that incentive pay is merely a political device to avoid paying more adequate base salaries and to sap teacher militancy on behalf of better pay. For this and other reasons, teachers' organizations have tended to emphasize the importance of better teacher selection and training and, once teachers pass their probation period, on the need for additional resources and greater discretionary authority for teachers. Criteria based upon the acquisition of credentials or scope of responsibilities rather than upon performance are favored.

*The Challenge to Professionalism and Occupational Security.* Singling out teachers for incentive pay carries additional negative connotations for teaching as a profession. A core tenet of a profession is that it assures through self-regulation in recruitment and training, as well as in actual performance, that the client's best interests will be served. Some teachers feel that their professional image is discredited by the notion that they have to be "bribed" to do good work.

Furthermore, if bonus pay for teachers alone is seen to be a necessary and sufficient means for achieving quality education, then the onus for whatever shortcomings characterize our educational system rests entirely or primarily upon the teacher. Teachers fear, not without cause, that they are likely to be the scapegoats for failures the responsibilities for which lie elsewhere, or are shared by others.

Resistance of teachers to an incentive plan partly reflects their concern about the educational audit which is necessary to it. There is great difficulty, even for objective and sophisticated investigators, in accurately isolating the contribution of each factor, including the teacher, to pupil learning. Moreover, at the heart of much of the resistance to any form of accountability is the recurrent issue of *who* will have access to such information and how it will be used. In addition, teachers are afraid, as already noted, that routine, standardized testing and the fixed curricula that it implies will erode professional prerogatives even further.

A long-term, and perhaps more fundamental, reservation is that an auditing procedure is likely to make possible cost-benefit analysis and to spur innovations in pedagogical technology, manpower, and organization. Teachers may be confronted with the development of highly specialized new occupational roles, most of which will require less or different qualifications. In addition, more extensive use is likely to be made of teaching machines, visual aids, and programmed materials that would permit the use of persons with lesser skill and ability. These changes would routinize and demystify teaching as a calling requiring special talent, training, and experience. Thus arises the latent fear that the teaching profession as we now know it will be rendered obsolete or, at least, that the demand for such positions will be markedly reduced. There is no assurance that teachers would not find themselves the victims of progress as have so many industrial workers in the past. A politically sophisticated teacher (or his organizational representatives) might understandably refuse to cooperate with a demonstration precisely because of its long-term implications. Thus, an incentive scheme tied to pupil performance is potentially a Pandora's box with an automatic time-delay fuse.

*Administrators and the School Governing Board: The View From the Top.* Most discussions of performance-based incentive plans for teachers take for granted that the school administrators and the school governing board can be counted upon to welcome it and to provide support necessary to assure its successful implementation. This, however, is not the case.

Such plans entail risks for administrators. The two major sources of constraints upon them consist, externally, of the school governing body and the constituency-at-large and, internally, of the teachers.

Although throughout much of this discussion we speak of administrators generally, we must acknowledge important differences among them, particularly, for our purposes, the principal and the superintendent. The principal, in an increasingly centralized school system, is typically deprived of real discretionary authority over important educational matters. He is primarily a custodian of people, time, and resources. Since pressure for educational excellence is typically low (for reasons which will be considered), the primary incentive for the principal is to maintain the organization without incident. Such a function is clearly jeopardized by innovation.

The situation of the superintendent is far different. He is appointed by the school board and presumably reflects its general consensus, inconsistent though it may often be. Although he is their agent in implementing their wishes in the school system, the board is, in practice, dependent upon him for their knowledge of technical pedagogical issues. For example, it is likely that, with respect to a teacher incentive plan, a school committee will be strongly influenced by the superintendent's views. The actual balance between them depends upon a variety of considerations, including characteristics of the community, the school, and the personal qualities of the superintendent, the board leadership, and even his subordinate administrators. [18, 23, 30]

Whatever the internal differences, the school administration overwhelmingly shares a preoccupation with organizational maintenance or survival. Superior educational performance has *not* been an important condition for survival. Unlike the private school, the public school has never been in real jeopardy of going out of business if its educational quality drops. A regular educational audit may deprive an administrator of a potentially effective means of internal control over his school, but it also provides him (and the teachers) with a margin of freedom from public accountability.

Few citizen governing boards develop a clear and consistent knowledge about and commitment to high-quality education. [2, 31] The aim of getting the best education that money can buy is likely to mean, in practice, getting the best that they choose to afford. The pressure to maintain a conservative fiscal posture, coupled with vague or conflicted goals, serves to diffuse consensus and undermine determination to optimize the quality of educational practice.

In the absence of an effective demand for educational excellence and a means for measuring it, the most salient press upon many administrators is often political: to minimize or neutralize the ever-present threat of "interference" in school affairs by the laity. There is a fine line between involvement and intrusion. Citizen participation requires access to strategic information about inputs, outputs, and outcomes. The right and the necessity to know, however, must avoid disruptive interference in day-to-day operations. Independent audits can help to maintain this distinction. In its absence, trust, always difficult to establish, becomes even more critical and tenuous. This problem is fairly universal, but is perhaps even more difficult in domains such as education which are more vulnerable to public scrutiny and pressure.

As a result, there are a number of strategies which administrators are likely to develop to minimize the risk of inappropriate and disruptive intrusion. One is the near-phobia about anything that is the least bit controversial or offensive; thus, the thrust towards conservatism. Without public support for improved educational performance, the value of innovation is reduced and the risks it entails in conflict and higher costs, enhanced.

Another strategem is restricting the number of persons who have access to information and the decision-making process, especially the public-at-large. ("Public relations" or "public information" are euphemisms for withholding strategic facts while deferring to the "right of the people to know.") This serves, particularly, to discourage the development of organized pressures that threaten to move *outside* the prescribed, "orderly" channels of educational governance.

However, there are also *internal* targets of secrecy: vital matters pertinent to policy-making are not usually shared with teachers. Teachers are not given a systematic opportunity, as a group, to consider major issues of the educational enterprise and to offer their advice, if not consent, about them. Such a process of participation, indeed, might begin to encourage a greater awareness and appreciation of organizational issues and enhance the effectiveness of the educational enterprise.

Against this background, the possible risks of a teacher-incentive plan for administrators become clear. The very proposal may precipitate controversy, conflict, and persistent cleavages by re-opening issues which were previously settled about educational goals and priorities. It should be borne in mind that many segments of the public, including interested parents, are typically unaware that an issue (or policy) is actively under consideration until after it manifests itself in practice. Furthermore, most people are not fully aware of the ultimate results of many issues which, at the time, appear insignificant and are left to be settled by relatively small numbers of people. Finally, those who run the schools fear endemic dissident groups who might seize upon some issue to provoke and escalate controversy for their own ulterior purposes.

There are many school governing bodies, especially in the inner city, that share the average administrator's concern about controversy and conflict. Many of these governing bodies represent a minority faction or social elite of a community and they are likely to assess any innovation, including incentive pay for teacher, in terms of its probable effect on their continued hegemony over the school committee. It is much easier for a small faction of incumbents to maintain themselves in power if the community is quiescent and, if there are no real issues which would arouse public interest and enlarge the size of the voting electorate. In most instances, such school boards are dominated by cost-conscious persons who have no children currently in school and who are likely to readily settle for an extremely modest-quality education. Occasionally, in a few of the more affluent suburbs, the governing bodies are dominated by social elites who have a strong commitment to superior education. They, too, jealously guard access to school board membership to minimize the chance of spokesmen who would too readily sacrifice quality education or favor an educational goal or means of which the dominant elite disapproves.

Administrators are concerned not only about the initial impact of the proposed incentive plan but its implications after it is underway. Innovations in teaching curriculum, staffing, and techniques always challenge cherished lay conceptions about pedagogy. Furthermore, such innovations are likely to entail higher cost outlays.[1]

Although an educational audit provides information essential for pupil evaluation and teacher payment, it also has the potential of being used for purposes of *system* evaluation. It not only provides the administrator with the means of holding his subordinates accountable for results, but it also makes him accountable (in the case of the principal) to his superiors and (for all administrators) to the school governing committee and to the public-at-large. A concern about the complexities of

1. Although the direct demonstration costs of innovations in school staffing and programming will be underwritten by outside funding, such costs are destined to continue when the demonstration is but a memory unless an effort is made to restore the educational situation to the *status quo ante*, not an easy matter to achieve.

interpretation and the risk of innocent or malicious distortion is one which the administrator shares with the teacher. Hence, in connection with a recent proposal in Massachusetts to undertake annual testing of reaching achievement throughout the state, principals as well as teachers relented in their opposition only when they were assured that access to the test results would be restricted to the superintendents of the school systems involved.

The ultimate attitude of administrators towards an incentive plan for teachers will be heavily influenced by what teachers think about it. Administrators and teachers are in a situation of mutual dependence, despite their difference in formal authority. Although teachers are accountable to their administrative superiors, they can exert decisive influence not only through their professional organizations but also in informal and covert ways by which subordinates can undermine or enhance the authority and effectiveness of superiors. In this respect, the principal, as a classic "man-in-the-middle," is much more vulnerable than the superintendent. Generally speaking, there is a covert, if not explicit, understanding between administrators and teachers to keep their disagreements and conflicts "within the family" and, at all costs, to avoid embroiling the public-at-large.

Administrators also are aware of the capacity of teachers to stimulate public controversy about a teacher-incentive plan, especially by raising issues affecting the implications for pupils. Hence, administrators must accede to an adamant teacher position even when, in principle, they may take exception to it, unless vital educational or political (survival) considerations are seriously compromised.

The attitude of administrators with respect to the proposed incentive plan will be affected by its implications for their traditional role. Implementation of such a plan is likely to contribute to decentralization of authority and responsibility. The delegation of authority is not without its price for the administrator, not only in the potential risks entailed, but also in the loss of prestige and pleasure in the exercise of power. (For the principal, of course, this will mean a measure of enfranchisement which he may share with teachers. This may not be, initially, an unmitigated boon since many principals [as well as teachers] are likely to be unprepared—by training, experience, or inclination—to exercise the leadership demands of their new role.)

The risk will increase because, presumably, one major impact of an incentive plan tied to pupil performance will be to spur a ceaseless search for teaching approaches that work. Such a ferment is bound to raise unpredictable problems. The day is likely to be filled not only with more decisions, but new kinds of decisions as well.

## Performance-contracting Revisited

Despite the fact that final outcomes are not yet available on the efficacy of financial incentive schemes, there is enough evidence, both within the educational domain as well as from other areas, that such plans have promise for inducing change. Indeed, the evidence appears powerful enough to justify the recommendation that a wide-scale, government-sponsored effort be mounted as a field demonstration.

However, the preceding discussion has raised an important caveat in appraising intramural performance-contracting as a means of improving pupil academic performance. It must be viewed as but one element in a system which itself is a critical intervening agent of change between the incentive scheme and pupil achievement. Although viewing a school organization as a structure of incentives is a useful analytic perspective, such a complex institution cannot be reduced to that alone. These and other considerations lead us to re-examine selected strategic issues about the target and form of incentives, the utility of complementary sources of supports for change, and the significance of such operational questions as the formula for calculating incentives.

### INCENTIVES FOR TEACHERS ALONE?

Singling out teachers as the focus of incentive pay deflects attention from the compelling reality that the failure of children to learn, a problem more commonly found among the poor and minority groups, is a *system* problem, rather than the failure of teachers alone. Although teachers are the ones who have the primary contact with pupils and mediate between them and other aspects of the educational environment, they are not the masters of their own fate, and are constrained by influences within and without the school—including their immediate principals, higher administrators, the governing school committee, etc.

Once this premise is clearly acknowledged—that the roots of educational failure, to the extent that it lies within the sphere of the school, is a *system* responsibility—then the question becomes one of enlisting the active support of *all* the participants to the educational enterprise.

In considering the structure of incentives important to each of the participants, emphasis is given to monetary devices only because of the flexibility which these afford to public policy.

*Principals and Administrators.* Although incentive pay may be less important than concerns about job promotions for principals and other executives (compared to teachers), it is not without relevance. There is no reason why, in addition to other incentives, *all* paid staff of a school (or school system) should not also be subject to the inducement of bonus pay tied to educational audit. An important advantage of such a plan encompassing all personnel would lie in its dramatizing the *system* nature of responsibility for educational failure, thus offsetting the invidious implications of singling out teachers. At worst, only a small fraction of personnel not directly involved in teaching target pupils would draw pay (adding, incidentally, only a small fraction to the total cost) as "free-loaders." More likely, this would spur advice, cooperation with, and support of the "front-line" teachers and perhaps create a genuine "system" where there had been none.

Measures designed to minimize the administrative inconvenience and financial costs associated with a performance-contracting plan for teachers also would reduce administrative resistance. Providing management-support services for principals and other executives would assist them with unforeseen contingencies and also minimize the unstated anxieties that are likely to be evoked by the prospect of any major administrative change. Hence, offering as an option consultation services before, during, and for a period after the close of a demonstration or major organizational innovation, would enhance the receptivity of the principal and other key administrators.

*The School Committee.* A school committee might be expected to endorse the concept of performance-linked incentive pay if this concept promises a gain both in educational quality and in organizational accountability. Furthermore, the notion of payment proportional to results might be expected to strike a responsive chord. However, there are certain counter-indications. From the perspective of most governing boards, there may be more risks and fewer advantages in such a scheme than are apparent to the casual observer. Given the nature of the fiscal base for public education, they are likely to be preoccupied with cost reduction.

As the earlier discussion implied, an incentive system, at least initially, will necessarily add to the total dollar outlay in two ways. First, the total salary budget will have to be greater if an incentive scheme is not to be introduced at the expense of the base salary structure. Furthermore, social and technological innovations may require an additional investment. Additional costs can be offset in two important ways: either by federal funding or by major gains in efficiency that conceivably might result.

Federal revenue-sharing has already been under active consideration; its adoption is only a matter of time. Cost reductions, as a result of a more productive learning environment, are not likely to occur at the outset. Instead, the prospect is for an *increased* budgetary outlay, but one which, hopefully, would be accompanied by a substantial *improvement* in the quality of education. Thus, although the total educational bill would initially rise, the *average* cost (calculated in terms of results) would go down. (Assume, for example, that a forty-billion-dollar outlay produces a 70% grade-level achievement while an additional four-billion-dollar investment [10%] yields a 100% grade level achievement.) Buying a better education may actually turn out to cost *less* than a mediocre one *if* the costs and benefits are measured in terms of the long run for the entire society. This is a sophisticated argument, and one likely to gain endorsement only if it can be supported by the results of an audit.

In addition, the immediate receptivity by the committee to intramural performance-contracting will depend greatly on the stance taken toward it by the school administration (especially the superintendent), and the nature of their relationship to each other. The lack of an independent audit makes the school committee even more dependent upon the administration. Under these circumstances, the committee and the administration are even less likely to risk the predictable opposition from teachers and the prospect of higher initial costs for the promise of uncertain payoffs in a remote future.

*Pupils.* One of the spinoff benefits of an incentive system for school personnel is that students are likely to receive more individual attention than usual. The consequence of this, hopefully, will be to accelerate academic achievement.

The question arises whether payment to students (extrinsic reward) is a necessary part of this scheme. While skill-mastery itself is an intrinsic motivation, the population of any particular school may require less subtle and more immediate forms of reinforcement. Whatever strategy is most applicable must remain in the jurisdiction of the school staff. The financial option, however, must be made available in order to provide the opportunity to set up whatever reward system is decided.

THE STRUCTURE OF PRIVATE INCENTIVES: INDIVIDUAL OR GROUP

Discussions of incentive-pay schemes typically assume that such incentives will be structured on an individual basis. Much of the ambivalence towards such a plan has to do with the negative implications of incentive pay in its individualistic form. Hence, consideration should be given to offering school personnel the option of a group incentive in which their pooled incentive earnings would be shared. [17, 24]

Such an alternative would encourage the coordination and integration of all efforts and resources: (1) by breaking down the various forces, including discipline boundaries, which isolate each category of school personnel; and (2) by encouraging innovations in programming and organization. At the same time, this permits some teachers and other staff to participate in the incentive who otherwise might be excluded.[2] A group incentive is also more suitable to schools in which team-teaching or similar arrangements already exist, thus making it impossible to disentangle the respective contributions of particular individuals to the learning process.

A group incentive has still other advantages. It has the potential of liberating a group *esprit de corps* that will activate extra effort and cooperation. Finally, a group incentive is likely to enhance discretionary authority and encourage initiatives of school personnel which, as individuals, they might be more reluctant to exercise.

Such a scheme, of course, is not without its problems. Although it is likely to minimize one major source of invidious comparison and friction, it may introduce others. There is always the issue of whether there are "freeloaders," staff who cannot or will not carry their own weight. In addition, if an incentive scheme is shared on an equal basis, some may argue that its motivational force is muted. There is no plan that is without its risks or disadvantages. On the balance, the advantages far outweigh the possible disadvantages. This is an issue which might well be left to the discretion of local schools or school systems to resolve. (The relative merits of various forms of an incentive is a question that would be appropriate to evaluate in a major demonstration project.)

DISCRETIONARY FUNDS

Discretionary funds, separate from incentive pay, might also

2. For example, an incentive pay plan focused on reading and which would be limited to the pupil's primary (or reading) teacher might also include other teachers as well—the art, music, and physical education. These teachers might systematically aim to reinforce the day's reading plan in each of their classes.

be made available to schools. No restriction should be placed on how such funds are to be used. They might be spent for staff training, for additional staff (*e.g.*, teacher aides), specialist services, materials, teaching machines, programs, or for other activities such as field trips. Such a contingency fund is not only instrumental but can have both symbolic and political implications.

The benefits of such funds should not be restricted just to children who may be the immediate target of a teacher-incentive plan; *e.g.*, children performing below grade level. For one thing, schools may prefer not to develop teaching methods unique to such children, or in other ways separate them from other children in the teaching process. Moreover, extending at least some benefits of an incentive scheme to *all* children would enhance the interest and the support of the effort toward performance-accountability on the part of parents whose children are *not* the primary target of remedial efforts.

Undoubtedly, there is a risk in making discretionary funds routinely available. They will be spent whether their use was really essential to improved pupil performance or not. They may thereby provide a distorted picture of the cost required to achieve performance-accountability. Furthermore, availability of gadgets and additional services may inadvertently deflect attention from more decisive issues affecting pupil performance—the organization of the school and the respective roles of administrators, teachers, pupils, and parents. This is another consideration which needs to be taken into account in designing an incentive plan.

An important issue is *who* is to decide and administer such discretionary funds. If the matter is left completely up to the local school, it is likely to mean that such decisions will be handled in ways customary to the particular school. This may mean a restricted voice in such matters for many principals, especially in highly centralized school systems, and for most teachers. Alternately, guidelines can at least specify that the authority over such funds rests with the individual school.

There are some advantages to earmarking a portion of such institutional funds for separate disposition by administrators (principal) and teachers: it may encourage initiative in teachers who otherwise might too readily defer to the principal. On the other hand, it is important to avoid actions that work at cross-purposes, and to constrain the administration and the teachers (along with parents) to work together in a more egalitarian manner by bolstering the teachers' authority on certain matters of policy. Such funds might be jointly administered by a "performance-contract planning council" that includes adequate representation for all faculty, preferably of their own choosing. (Parents might well be included on such a council.)

Discretionary funds can be dispensed on the basis of collective decisions or for collective purposes. On the other hand, funds can also be allotted for individual teacher and administrative discretionary use. This is the kind of issue that is best left to the local school.

Such funds can be allotted either in a fixed amount calculated on a per capita basis or be tied to the results of an educational audit. In the latter case, this would become an organizational incentive analogous to the private incentive. Although organizational funds tied to results may afford a more powerful incentive to achievement, they are also likely to be self-defeating: schools with the least difficult problems and the most effective staff will, in time, enjoy more adequate resources than schools with the most acute needs. Thus, the inequalities among schools already characteristic of our public schools will be further reinforced. Although the *organizational* incentive is an interesting variable, we strongly incline to favor a fixed discretionary fund.

The amount of such funds is arbitrary. It should be enough to support essential changes as needed in curriculum materials, as well as other reasonable innovations.

THE FORMULA FOR BONUS PAY

Although incentive pay, as a lever for behavioral change,

appears sound in principle, its effectiveness in practice
depends a great deal on what often appear to be purely technical and sometimes highly trivial details. The formula for the
calculation of bonus pay provides an illustration of important
policy issues implicit in seemingly trivial technical issues.

*The Adequacy of Payoffs.* A fundamental question about
any incentive scheme is how much for how many. The choice
between a schedule of high payoffs to a few, or modest payoffs
to many, depends on a number of assumptions about the participants and their objectives. The latter formula appears preferable in light of the considerations discussed previously. A formula which diffuses an incentive to the largest number of
school personnel is most likely to raise the level of performance
of the *average* teacher and, at the same time, minimize the
potentially invidious aspects of the plan. A scheme of widespread benefits also is more consistent with newer assumptions
about the nature of effective teaching and learning: that it
is heavily influenced by complex *system* forces that require
collaboration.

*Diffusion of Benefits Among Children.* The nature of the
particular payoff formula will also affect the pattern of diffusion
of educational benefits among children. A formula which
rewards teachers for individual learning gains among pupils
may inadvertently result in selective attention by teachers to
pupils who show the best prospects for a large and prompt
improvement. *Averaging* pupil performance, on the other
hand, is a means for assuring that children who present more
difficult or challenging problems are not neglected. The important point is that special attention needs to be given to the
specific formula to make sure it will realize the intended educational objectives.

### Are Incentives Enough?

A monetary incentive scheme tied to an educational audit is
a peer-oriented model for achieving performance accountability: it relies upon a financial incentive to provide sufficient
impetus to overcome past inertia to change. However, whether

or not it is successful depends upon what it really takes to reach children effectively who have been under-achievers. The assumption has been made that more will be required of the school than simply "trying harder." These learning problems manifested by children of the poor and socially disadvantaged minority groups in contemporary schools are deeply rooted in the conditions of the larger society—in poverty and inequality, and in early socialization experiences reinforced by subsequent socio-environmental influences. Thus, they will require that schools do things very differently. A performance-contracting scheme offers limited prospects of success so long as the results of educational audits are restricted to teachers and administrators, as, in some places, they are insisting. The educational system is unlikely to change without *external* sources of pressure, despite the presence of a growing minority of teachers and administrators oriented towards reform. A performance-contracting scheme involving incentive pay and an educational audit has the potential of enlarging this *internal* constituency for change. However, only sustained *outside* pressure is likely to produce and maintain an internal dynamic for performance-accountability. Massive fiscal support of local schools (through revenue-sharing, for example) by the federal government, linked to a policy of performance-contracting and educational audits, constitutes one such possible effective external source of constraint. Equal if not more important, however, is the continuous presence of forceful and determined neighborhood residents and parents to stimulate and bolster such changes. Mobilizing a more effective parent constituency through the schools has long-term consequences, as well, in that it generates an organized popular base of support for federal, state, and local programs on behalf of education. Hence, the vital importance, as a step towards performance-accountability, of re-inserting parents, who have the most direct and immediate stake in results, into the decision-making process in a more effective and constructive fashion. The possibility of educational auditing and performance-contracting will contribute to this. [11, 22, 27, 28]

Even assuming, however, that school superintendents discreetly share results of the audit with their respective school committees (and, even less likely, with the local parent-teacher associations, or parent councils), the nature of these particular parent and citizen groups do not offer optimistic ground for achieving a new major thrust towards school reform. The structure of governance must also be modified in such a way that the balance of control moves from the current provider-dominated system to a citizen-controlled system strongly committed to better education. A shift in the focus of accountability from inputs to results involves a major change; its prospects are improved if a multi-level strategy is involved which, at least, includes an educational audit, staff incentive pay, discretionary funds, and an effective citizen governing body.

## Summary and Conclusions

This paper has considered financial incentives for teachers tied to pupil performance as a strategy for achieving educational accountability in the public schools. Incidentally, there are alternative models for accomplishing the same result that also rely on an incentive principle. The best known of these models is the voucher system which attempts, through creating effective parent purchasing power, to rejuvenate the traditional competitive market mechanism. A comparison of the alternative incentive plans is useful, but beyond the scope of this paper.

An incentive plan singling out teachers is systematically examined from the perspective of the major participants in the educational institution: the pupils, the teachers, the administrators, and the school committee, representing a citizen constituency. Such a plan, despite its initial appeal, is likely to have a very limited impact so long as it is restricted to teachers. It offers promise as a significant catalytic agent of change only if it is part of a relatively integrated *system* or series of *sub-systems*. In the context of the school, this means, among other things, taking into account the other major participants besides the teacher: the administrator, the staff specialist, and the pupil, who contribute significantly to educational outcomes. In short, there is a need, at the very least, to conceptualize a school as a "system of incentives." (In this connection, a comprehensive view would include the full range of incentives, non-pecuniary as well as pecuniary ones.) However useful such a perspective is as a dynamic element, it does not exhaust the other important properties of an organization: the role of pedagogical and organizational ideology, norms, patterns of social structure, and technology, each of which exerts some autonomous influence on pupil educational outcomes.

The main thrust of this analysis centered upon the *internal* system of the school. However, it is equally essential to consider the larger environment which impinges upon the school and its participants. Included in this framework are federal, state, and local governmental agencies, and a citizen constituency. (The analytic framework and the level of systems perspective will determine whether the school community and parents, as a collective, are considered as part of the internal or external system of the school. From our vantage point, the school community [and parents] are external to the individual school.) If an incentive scheme is to be successfully introduced into the school and contribute to a dynamic thrust towards accountability, there is a critical need to maintain an *external* as well as an internal pressure for change. The federal government, providing massive funding, linked to specific policies and guidelines, can provide an important spur to innovation. Such an impetus, however, will be substantially reinforced if linked to more effective participation by citizen constituencies—especially parents—whose strong commitment to quality education counter-balances local preoccupation with costs.

## References

1. Blascke, Charles, *Educational Turnkey News*, 1970, p. 1.

2. Bloomberg, Warner, Jr., and Kincaid, John, "Parent Participation: Practical Policy or Another Panacea?" *Urban Review*, V. 2, No. 7, June 1967.

3.  Borich, Gary, ed., *Accountability* (special issue of *Journal of Research and Development in Education*, V. 5, No. 1, Fall, 1971).

4.  Bowers, C. A., "Accountability From a Humanistic Point of View," *The Educational Forum*, V. 35, No. 4, May, 1971, pp. 479-486.

5.  Brenton, Myron, *What's Happened to Teacher*, New York: Avon Books, Coward-McCann, Inc., 1971.

6.  Clark, Peter B., and Wilson, James Q., "Incentive Systems: A Theory of Organizations," *Administrative Science Quarterly*, V. 6, No. 2, 1961, pp. 129 - 166.

7.  Coleman, James, et al., *Equality of Educational Opportunity*, Washington, D.C.: U.S. Department of Health Education, Superintendent of Documents Catalogue No. FS 5.238:38001, National Center for Educational Statistics, 1966.

8.  Council for Basic Education, "How One Ghetto School Achieves Success in Reading," *Reprint Bulletin*, V. 13, No. 6, February, 1969.

9.  Elam, Stanley, "The Age of Accountability Dawns in Texarkana," *Phi Delta Kappan*, 1970.

10.  "Evaluating Teacher Performance," *Educational Research Service*, Circular No. 3, May, 1969, pp. 1 - 62.

11.  Fantini, Mario D., "Participation, Decentralization, Community Control, and Quality Education," *The Record*, V. 71, No. 1, September, 1969.

12.  Gordon, Edmund W., and Wilkerson, Doxey A., *Compensatory Education for the Disadvantaged*, New York: College Entrance Examination Board, 1966.

13.  Goslin, David, *Teachers and Testing*, New York: Russell Sage Foundation, 1967.

14.  Herndon, James, *The Way It's Spozed To Be*, New York: Simon and Schuster, 1968.

15.  Hunter, Lloyd, and Rogers, Frederick, "Testing: Politics and Pretenses," *Urban Review*, December, 1967.

16.  "Interview with Albert Shanker," *Urban Review*, November, 1969, pp. 19 - 27.

17.  Johnson, Richard, and Frederickson, Ronald, "Effect of Financial Remuneration and Case Description on Counselor Perform-

ance," *Journal of Counselling Psychology*, V. 15, March, 1968, pp. 130 - 135.

18. Koerner, James D., *Who Controls American Education*, Boston: Beacon Press, 1968.

19. Lessinger, Leon, "Accountability in Education," *National Committee for Support of Public Schools Bulletin*, February, 1970, pp. 4 - 6.

20. Lessinger, Leon, "After Texarkana, What?" *Nation's Schools*, V. 84, No. 6, December, 1969, pp. 37 - 40.

21. Lieberman, M., "An Overview of Accountability," *Phi Delta Kappan*, V. 52, No. 4, December, 1970, pp. 194 - 195.

22. Lopate, Carol; Flexman, Erwin; Bynam, Effie M.; and Gordon, Edmund W., "Decentralization and Community Participation in Public Education," *Review of Educational Research*, V. 40, No. 1, pp. 135 - 151.

23. Masters, Nicholas A.; Salisbury, Robert H.; and Elliot, Thomas H., *State Politics and the Public Schools: An Exploratory Analysis*, New York: Alfred A. Knopf, 1964.

24. Melman, Seymour, *Decision-making and Productivity*, New York: John Wiley and Sons, Inc., 1953.

25. Miles, Matthew B., *Innovation in Education*, New York: Bureau of Publications, Teachers College, Columbia University, 1964.

26. Miles, Matthew B., "Some Properties of Schools as Social Systems," in Watson, Goodwin, ed.s., *Change in School Systems*, Washington, D.C.: N.E.A., Cooperative Project for Educational Development, National Training Laboratories.

27. Miller, S. M., and Rein, Martin, "Participation, Poverty, and Administration," *Public Administration Review*, V. 29, No. 1, January - February, 1969.

28. Oscarson, Janice M., "Community Involvement in Accountability," in Borich, Gary, ed., *Accountability* (special issue of *Journal of Research and Development in Education*, V. 5, No. 1, Fall, 1971).

29. Ryan, William, *Blaming the Victim*, New York: Pantheon Books, Random House Publishers, 1971.

30. Schrag, Peter, *Village School Downtown*, Boston: Beacon Press, 1967.

31.  Seldon, David, "School Decentralization: A Positive Approach," *The Record*, V. 71, No. 1, September, 1969, pp. 85 - 92.

32.  Tyler, Ralph, "The Problems and Possibilities of Educational Evaluation," *The Schools and the Challenge of Innovation* (Supplementary paper by Research and Policy Committee for Economic Development), New York: McGraw-Hill, Inc., 1969, pp. 76 - 90.

33.  Watson, Goodwin, "Resistance to Change," in Watson, Goodwin, ed., *Change in School Systems*, Washington, D.C.: N.E.A., Cooperative Project for Educational Development, National Training Laboratories.

34.  Weber, George, and Marmon, William, *Merit Pay and Alternatives: Descriptions of Some Current Programs*, Washington, D.C.: Monograph, Council for Basic Education, May, 1969.

# IV

## Welfare

Martin Rein *is professor of urban studies and planning at Massachusetts Institute of Technology. Born in New York, he received a B.A. from Brooklyn College, the Master of Science in Social Work from Columbia University, and the Ph.D. from Brandeis University. Before coming to MIT, he served as Professor in Bryn Mawr College's Graduate Department of Social Work and Social Research. In addition, he has been a lecturer or associate at such diverse institutions as Brandeis University, University of Pittsburgh School of Social Work, Albert Einstein College of Medicine, University of Pennsylvania School of City Planning, and the Centre for Environmental Research in London. Dr. Rein's work has dealt extensively with problems of poverty, social planning, and social policy, and he is the author of numerous books and articles on these subjects.*

# 7

# Work Incentives and Welfare Reform in Britain and the United States

## MARTIN REIN

There is no consensus about the essential features of a negative or reverse income tax (NIT). Three criteria can be identified: the higher the income the lower the benefits; income alone is the test of eligibility and no work test is imposed; and benefits bear a close relationship to the tax system. Turning from theory to practice we find that some countries have been reluctant to embrace all three principles, but some have accepted the idea of earnings-retention. Basically, if this principle is to encourage employment it must avoid penalizing those who earn income with an equivalent decline in benefits, by permitting some retention of benefits as earnings rise. The greater the proportion of earnings retained, the stronger the work incentive. In this paper we accept earnings- or benefit-retention as a sufficient criterion for establishing an incomplete negative income tax. However, even the use of similar principles of income-testing and earning can serve different purposes and yield dramatically different outcomes. In Britain, negative taxation considered as earnings-retention has since 1970 been applied to the working poor in a program called Family Income Supplements (FIS); and in the United States since 1967, the NIT has been used to make work attractive to present recipients of welfare. This paper reviews the experience when the principle of the negative income tax is applied to the

151

different purposes of relieving economic distress and changing work-oriented behavior.*

These competing purposes of social policy are themselves of general significance. Public expenditure analysts distinguish between subsidies and transfers. A subsidy is a transaction designed to change behavior in the private sector. By contrast, a transfer extends consumption for its own sake and does not expect a direct *quid* for a *quo*. Some programs, transfer-subsidies, seek both aims. President Nixon's Family Assistance Plan (FAP) and House of Representatives Bill I (H.R. I) must be defined as a mixed transfer-subsidy. The British FIS, on the other hand, is a straightforward transfer. This paper may therefore be interpreted as a review of policies that demand reciprocity (benefits which are extended to alter behavior and are created to establish a positive incentive for work) and those which are unilateral transactions, designed to augment consumption and relieve distress. Some would argue that no policy for the poor may appropriately be viewed as a unilateral transfer. They are also designed to encourage social compliance, promote conformity, or facilitate achievement. The relief of distress, in this perspective, always serves some broader purpose of society, such as quelling discontent or subsidizing low wages,[1] hence the distinction between subsidies and transfers is misleading. I reject this view, and instead want to argue that differences in legislative intent are fateful for program outcomes. In particular I will try to argue that subsidies which purport to change the behavior and attitudes of individuals have different consequences from transfers to consumers. Attempts to change personal behavior through subsidies in the United States prove too costly to sustain, and gradually they surrender to administrative and coercive policies. In Britain, on the other hand, the cumulative effect of multiple transfer has led to some measure of income-

*I wish to acknowledge with thanks the help of Alan Sager in drafting an earlier version of this paper. I also wish to thank Leonard Hausman and Tony Atkinson for their comments.

1. Frances Fox Piven and Richard Cloward, *Regulating the Poor*, New York: Pantheon Press, 1970.

equalization between the poor and not-so-poor. However, the income gap between the top and the average is widening. Thus, attempts to evaluate the merits of any combined system of negative income tax and means-tested benefits should consider not only the system itself but also the purposes—transfer or subsidy—for which it is employed.

After defining the context of the discussion by setting out some brief definitions, the paper will proceed to describe recent American and British experiences with the NIT and means-tested benefits. Finally, the two cases will be compared and implications for policy considered.

BACKGROUND TO THE U.S. EXPERIENCE

In the past ten years from 1962 to 1972, federal policy has tried to discover a way of reducing the rise in welfare case-loads and cost. A review of the history of these efforts suggests that three main strategies were pursued: a service strategy, an incentive strategy, and a restrictive strategy. Each of these elements are found in the major changes to the Social Security Act in 1962, 1967, and in the administration's 1970 abortive proposals for the Family Assistance Plan (FAP) and the 1971 Ways and Means Committee bill H.R. 1, not yet implemented into law. In the course of the decade, as the argument for incentives has proved politically unacceptable because of the high costs involved in its implementation, policy has increasingly embraced the service and restrictive approaches.

THE 1962 AMENDMENTS

The 1962 amendments were heralded as the services amendments. This approach emphasized problem-identification first; then making available to welfare recipients information, advice, and referral to other community resources; and finally direct help through specific services such as day-care. These activities were designed to encourage "prevention and rehabilitation" as a way of reducing the size of the case-loads. While casework (diagnosis, advice, and referral) played a prominent role in these services, the emphasis on manpower training was not neglected, as the Community Work and Training (CW&T) program attests. The beginnings of incentive strategy can be also recognized, since Congress permitted states to allow work expenses as an incentive to encourage welfare mothers to seek employment. The incentive approach was part of a wider income strategy which emphasized broader coverage, larger grants, abandonment of the categories, and simplification of eligibility determination. Essentially it sought a less conditional claim to assistance and emphasized uniformity of treatment of clients. Above all, it sought an economic improvement in family circumstance when employment and welfare were combined.

The restrictive strategy took several forms. In part it was focused on quality control, a new method of reviewing a random sample of eligibility decisions made by caseworkers to determine the percentage of incorrect decisions. Here the assumption was that rolls could be reduced if the eligibility decisions were more stringently reviewed. The Senate Appropriations Committee in the spring of 1962 demanded a survey of rates of ineligibles on state rolls to be accomplished in the following fiscal year. The Federal Department of HEW had simultaneously to make plans for a national eligibility survey while it was drafting the service regulations, illustrating, as Charles Gilbert points out, the "program's basic ambivalence."[2] A second approach was to make it more difficult for deserting fathers to avoid supporting their children and thus reduce eligibility by taking the financial reward out of desertions. Even in the Community Work and Training Program there were some elements of compulsion as some families were required by states to enter this program or lose their benefits.

THE 1967 AMENDMENTS

In 1967 much more attention was given to the incentive strategy. Indeed, it was the incentive approach contained in

2. Charles Gilbert, Swarthmore College, unpublished manuscript on the development of the social service amendments, n.d.

the "$30-1/3 rule," which permits recipients to keep the first $30 per month in earnings plus one-third of the balance, and in the expansion of deductions for work-related expenses that seems to reflect the main spirit of these amendments. But, again, a service provision was initiated, but now with emphasis on child-care and birth-control. The legislation was also restrictive; it required compulsory work-training programs for AFDC mothers and older children out of school. Those judged able to work or qualified for training were required to accept jobs, if available, or placement in the Department of Labor's Work Incentive Program (WIN). Moreover, the law established a freeze on welfare expenditures. The "freeze" limited federal support for cases based on family breakup to the proportion of the total state AFDC case-load formed by such cases in the first quarter of 1968. It was designed to encouraged the states to develop manpower and service programs, that is, to take positive action to reduce its AFDC caseload. But the "freeze" never went into effect. In addition, new relationships between welfare and law enforcement agencies were mandate to check desertion.

FAP

In August 1969 the President proposed the Family Assistant Plan (FAP), a bill which failed to pass in the Senate. The incentive strategy was carried still further by reducing the marginal tax rate from 67 to 50 percent, while providing an income guarantee of $1,600. Work-related services continued to be emphasized. A separate fund was set aside for day-care expenses; special provision was made to create 200,000 public employment jobs.[3] As total expenditure for services increased, provision was made to limit the amount of services per recipient to $2,000 per year. FAP also contained an expanded set of restrictive regulations which took the form of work rules and "suitable work" definitions.

3. These jobs, however, were not intended as permanent and regular. The circumstances of each job-holder would be reviewed every six months to

(Continued on p. 156)

FAP - OFF

In 1971 a modified version of FAP was introduced by the Ways and Means Committee and placed first on the congressional agenda. H.R. 1, like its predecessor, passed in the House, but by April 1972 it still languished in the Senate Finance Committee for lack of support. The bill increased the guarantee level from $1,600 to $2,400, but weakened incentives. The marginal tax rate was raised from 50 to 67 percent, established a fixed amount for work-related expenses, and eliminated the practice of paying social-security and income taxes for welfare recipients who obtained employment. All AFDC recipients were to be divided into two groups. Those able to work or acquire training would be assigned to the Opportunities for Families program (OFF), administered by the Department of Labor. Those unable to work, including families with young children under age six, would enroll in the Family Assistance Plan (FAP), administered by the Department of HEW. Distrustful of caseworkers' discretion, H.R. 1 developed explicit formal criteria of employability.

During the decade of legislative experimentation bent on reducing the size and cost of the AFDC case-load, a noticeable shift in emphasis appears to have emerged. While all three strategies of service, incentives, and restrictions remain, more stress appears now to be placed upon restriction. Some critics of H.R. 1 now believe that the primary purpose of the bill is "not to improve the well-being and dignity of the beneficiary, but to so control and harass his behavior at every point that he . . . will be either coerced into conformity or driven from the program altogether."[4] But one does not need to accept

---

determine whether a more appropriate position could be secured for him or her on a regular payroll. This emphasis on the transitional nature of the job must be interpreted, in part, as a safeguard against the displacement of regular public workers from their jobs and a prevention against permanent make-work assignments for relief recipients. These jobs may therefore be better regarded as social services.

4. *Welfare Law News*, Vol. 1, No. 4, Nov. 1971, Center on Social Welfare Policy and Law, N.Y.

so sharp a repudiation of H.R. 1 to recognize that the incentive strategy it proposes is weaker than that already accepted in the 1969 Social Security Amendments. Moreover, the services strategy has been of limited effectiveness in a period of high unemployment: witness the steady increase in the waiting list of WIN graduates awaiting job placement. Meanwhile caseloads and costs have continued to rise. Thus, a retreat from the incentives approach appears to have emerged, and more stress has been placed on restriction. Faith in services continues as the aim of reducing the size of the rolls has not only persisted but grown more insistent. How can we account for the shifting priorities? I believe that part of the explanation is related to the inherent contradictions in pursuing three related but incompatible aims: reducing poverty, promoting work incentives, and containing costs. No one of these aims can be forsaken; while other objectives such as fiscal relief to states must also be taken into account.

NEGATIVE TAXATION AND WORK INCENTIVES

American reformers had devised an incentive strategy which they hoped could alter the work behavior of those on welfare. The strategy was based on the assumption that people would work if they were economically better off and this motive alone could be sufficient to promote work-oriented behavior. The crucial task then was to revise the present welfare system so that this principle could be implemented.[5] The strategy was simple and compelling. Families who have no income from any sources would receive an allowance the value of which would vary based only on family size (not composition, *i.e.*, children of different ages would not receive different benefits, nor were there to be economies of scale such that larger families received proportionately less).

5. Of course, people could not work if there were no jobs, so full employment had to be accepted as a critical assumption as well; nor could they work if they lacked skills, so training seemed important; nor could they work without supportive services to care for their children while they were not at home, so child-care had to be provided. By itself the incentive strategy was incomplete. It had to be supplemented with services and jobs.

As income from earnings rises the level of benefits declines, but it declines at a lower rate than the increase from earnings; thus the family is economically better off when at work because it can keep some part of its earnings. The strategy assumes that "economic man" responds to the level of total income, rather than the stability of income. This argument does not consider that lower welfare payments might still be more attractive than higher earnings if the welfare income was dependable and stable. Income from working may be less attractive if it is erratic. If welfare were as easy to get on to as it is to get off, then the stability of eanings would play a less important part in choosing a higher rather than a more stable income. The crucial factor in the strategy was the rate at which benefits declined as income from other sources (especially income from employment) was augmented. This marginal tax rate held the key to the work incentive strategy since it was assumed that it could contribute to a higher level of total income which was, in principle, more important in governing work behavior than the stability of income.

THE DILEMMAS OF THE AMERICAN INCENTIVE STRATEGY

However compelling and persuasive the argument may be that an incentive strategy can alter the work behavior of recipients and thereby make welfare a self-liquidating program, in practice the strategy leads to intractable dilemmas that compel greater reliance upon administrative solutions. The principal dilemma arises because a single goal is seldom pursued in isolation from other equally desirable aims. In addition to trying to provide strong incentives for the poor to work without discouraging those already on the job, public policy hoped also to secure a decent basic allowance for those on welfare, along with a low rate of taxation on earned income (to encourage work), without raising total costs of the program to unsupportable heights. To encourage work, to reduce poverty, and to contain costs are incompatible aims. The task of coordinating the work-incentive features of the negative income tax with other autonomous means-tested programs to avoid problems of notches and discouragingly high marginal rates of taxation poses additional political and financial problems. There are three problems:

*Providing strong incentives for the poor to work without discouraging those already on the job.* The incentive strategy for welfare recipients becomes a disincentive for the working poor when the economic position of those who receive both welfare benefits and wages rises above the level of income which the working poor can command on the market, after taxes and work-related expenses are taken into account. Many of those at work may therefore be better off leaving their job, waiting whatever transitional period is necessary for securing welfare, and then combining work and welfare. Indeed, the whole strategy of encouraging welfare recipients to work becomes self-defeating if it simultaneously encourages the working poor to seek welfare. Hence, it was crucial to include the working poor in the proposed reform. "It is the only way," explained the Secretary of HEW to the Senate Finance Committee, "to prevent the low-wage worker from dropping into welfare."[6]

The inclusion of the working poor, however, inflates the numbers of persons eligible for benefits. The FAP proposal set forth by the President in August 1969 would have created a welfare population of 14 percent of all families. The more generous basic allowance and lower tax rate combination proposed by Senator Ribicoff would extend benefits to one-third of the total U.S. population by 1977. Such wide coverage was the unintentional but inevitable result of a system which provided both decent minimal benefits and work incentives to those on welfare. But because the working poor had to be included in the program, they benefited from the strong incentives designed for welfare families. Although some attempt was made to limit costs by excluding them from automatic eligibility to Medicaid and other benefits, this created new inequities which left those on welfare better off than those

6. U.S. Congress, Senate Committee on Finance. *Hearings on Family Assistance Act of 1970.* 91st Congress, 2nd Session, Part 1, 1970, p. 254.

at work. Consequently, the cost of including the working poor under the welfare reform strained the program's ability to serve the twin aims of adequate allowances and incentives to work.

*Securing a decent basic allowance to those on welfare, along with a low rate of taxation on earned income, without prohibitively raising the cost of the program.* Two factors drive the costs up: 1) the level of the basic allowance, which permits people with no income to avoid destitution, and 2) the strength of the work-incentive provisions, which enable people to retain a higher fraction of their earnings. The reasons are straightforward. A higher basic allowance at any given marginal tax rate must increase the income cutoff point where people are no longer eligible for benefits.[7] Because of the shape of the income distribution curve, each equal increase in the break-even point makes successively larger numbers of families eligible for benefits. Costs can be contained while increasing the basic allowance, but only by raising the marginal tax rate until the tax is 100 percent. This is, after all, the logic of the present welfare system. It is directed at the relief of distress rather than the encouragement of work. It is possible to neglect the problem of work incentives if we assume that the program serves primarily those outside the labor force. And this, after all, was the argument advanced by those who defended established practice. Welfare aids those without work potential (blind, disabled, aged, and families with dependent children). Hence even a generous system has little work incentive effects because eligibles cannot work even if they wanted to. Critics of the present system rejected the argument by declaring that families with children should be at work.

Costs increase as the marginal tax rate is lowered, essentially for the reasons reviewed above—more families can receive aid because the break-even point must, by the logic of the scheme, be raised. But costs can be contained by lowering

7. The basic formula that expresses the fixed relationship between the basic allowance (A), the break-even level (B), and the tax rate (t), is $A = tB$. The basic allowance is the product of the tax rate and the break-even level.

the basic allowance. The same break-even point of, say, $3,000 can be achieved by having a basic allowance of $1,000, 1,500, 2,000, or 3,000. This is made possible by simply altering the tax rate from one-third, to one-half, to two-thirds or finally to 100 percent. In this example, the cost of the scheme is about the same, but there is a trade-off between the poverty and work-incentive objectives. The combination of a low tax rate and a low allowance is more work-oriented than a higher allowance and a higher tax rate. In other words, cost-consciousness may make it attractive to sacrifice the objective of reducing poverty. A much lower basic allowance would be politically unacceptable because it must make many of those currently on welfare worse off than they presently are. But keeping the allowance level high enough to approach present welfare benefits levels, leads to total costs that rise sharply because costs are especially sensitive to changes in the tax rate. The crucial factor is the break-even point, and lower tax rates raise that point. "A plan with a 30 percent tax rate and a $1,600 basic allowance, for example, is somewhat more costly than a plan with a 70 percent tax rate and a $2,800 basic allowance."[8] This occurs because, in the first example, the cut-off point is $5,300, and in the latter case it is only $4,000. There is a choice, then, between lower and higher tax rates and allowances. The first approach sacrifices the poverty objective and the second the work-incentive approach.

Consider a less hypothetical example. The administration was under great pressure from liberals to raise the basic allowance guarantee. After all, no family can live on $1,600 a year. Subsequently, the level was raised in 1971 to $2,400 a year for a family of four. However, if the original tax rate of 50 percent were continued, a $2,400 basic allowance, combined with a $720 exemption, allows the family to have an income from earnings of $5,520 before being ineligible for welfare. This contrasts with the $3,920 cutoff point under the original

8. Jodie T. Allen, "A Funny Thing Happened on the Way to Reform," #301 - 14 Urban Institute, Oct. 15, 1971, p. 13.

FAP. Such a scheme has disastrous effects on the scope and cost of the program, since over 20 percent of the 52 million American families have incomes of less than $5,520. An increased allowance of $800 (from $1,600 to $2,400), while retaining the same tax rate triples the cost of the program. Conscious of the costs and forced politically to accept the aim of reducing poverty, it was the work-incentive objective which had to be diminished, and the tax rate was reluctantly raised to 67 percent. The perverse effect of this change was to create a situation where the work-incentive reforms already law under the 1967 amendments, even while retaining the same tax rate, were more generous than the proposed new reforms which were promoted as a strong work-incentive program. The "disregard" and work-expenses provisions accounted for the main difference. In the earlier legislation, $30 and one-third of the remaining monthly *gross* salary is disregarded and work expenses are reimbursed as incurred. This dilemma can be avoided only if higher costs and a larger welfare population are accepted.

Many congressmen who accept both the objective of relieving distress and encouraging work-oriented behavior by economic incentives are reluctant to accept the consequences that such policies imply. In the Senate Finance Committee debate on H.R. 1 Senator Curtis (R-Neb.), armed with information prepared for him by staff of HEW, confronted Senator Ribicoff, a proponent of higher basic allowance and lower tax rates, with a startling estimate. Curtis stated that if the basic allowance were gradually raised from a $3,000 guarantee level to $4,000, a 60 percent tax rate applied, recipients exempted from social-security and income taxes, and changes in the basic allowance were raised to take account of inflation, by 1977 one-third of the population of the United States would be on welfare. The Curtis dilemma is contained in the arithmetic of the negative income tax. It cannot be avoided. It does not appear politically feasible to accept so large a proportion of the total population on welfare, nor to forsake the objective of reducing poverty, or to abandon the goal of maintaining normal market incentives for work effort. It follows therefore that the only other approach available is to rely upon administrative devices to stimulate work effort among the poor. Bureaucratic solutions are substituted for the incentive of a low tax rate.

Some analysts have also recognized the problem that retrograde work incentives have been proposed under the rhetoric of strong work incentives. Jodie Allen, a research associate at the Urban Institute, reluctant to "return to the old welfare strategy of reliance on bureaucratic compulsion to stimulate work" has proposed a lower basic allowance. Allen compares three plans at different guarantee levels ranging from $2,800 to $3,200 and concludes that "Since the great majority of *working poor families* have more than $2,000 of earned income, they will generally be better off with a program with a relatively low basic guarantee and a low marginal tax than under a program with a higher basic guarantee and a high marginal tax."[9] But even the plan with the lowest allowances would cost from $20—30 billion, depending on disregards and the treatment of social-security and income taxes. Given these cost contrasts, it becomes clear why compulsion becomes a substitute for the incentive of a low tax rate.

*Coordinating the work-incentive features of the negative income tax with other means-tested programs.* The problem of the "poverty trap" has its origin in administrative arrangements which treat welfare in isolation from the family of means-tested programs of which it is a part. The difficulties of integrating the broader universe of means-tested programs creates two stubborn dilemmas: a notch problem, and a high cumulative marginal tax rate problem. These difficulties undermine the work-incentive approach. A notch creates a situation in which a family is economically worse off as its earnings increase; this arises when the family is subjected to more than a 100 percent tax rate. "High cumulative tax rates" refers to the increase in the tax rate as a result of the cumulative effect

9. Jodie Allen, "Alternatives to H.R. 1," mimeo, p. 3.

of recovering benefits or imposing taxes from several different programs.

A welfare family might in principle receive, in addition to welfare payments, a variety of goods and services which can be converted to a cash-equivalent value. These include housing, child-care, medical care, and food. Moreover, under the present legislation, welfare recipients are reimbursed for the social-security and income taxes they contribute. Families who are not at work do not incur such expenses as transportation to the job, eating meals away from home, extra clothing, etc. When the Senate Finance Committee, in 1971, reviewed the proposal for welfare reform submitted by the President (FAP), it severely criticized the program because it created a serious notch problem, whereby people were actually worse off economically if they went out to work. FAP then called for a $1,600 guarantee and 50 percent tax rate.

In the revised version of FAP (which the Senate Finance Committee rejected) and in the most recent version of H.R. 1, the administration tried to address the notch problem as best it could: by cashing out the value of food stamps and increasing the basic allowance from $1,600 to $2,400; by altering eligibility and benefits received from Medicaid.

However, the administration could not at the same time lower the marginal tax rate sufficiently to create the positive work incentives which make it economically worthwhile for welfare recipients to seek employment. Secretary of HEW Richardson makes the choice explicit in his testimony before the House Ways and Means Committee:

> The Committee will have to decide whether it placed the higher premium on the elimination of any cutoff point at which an individual's income drops, in order to have a steeper incentive line before that, or, to do what we have recommended, which is to flatten the incentive line in order to eliminate the notches.[10]

Two new problems arose. By cashing out the food stamps

10. U.S. Congress, Senate Committee on Finance, *Hearings on H.R. 16311*, 91st Congress, 2nd session, part 2, Washington, D.C.: U.S. Government Printing Office, August 1970, p. 301.

and raising the basic allowance to $2,400, a 50 percent tax rate would have yielded a break-even point of $5,520, which would be costly, because so many more families earn incomes up to this level than to the initially proposed break-even point of $3,700. Thus, efforts to solve the notch problem created cost difficulties. H.R.1 tried to resolve the cost problems by raising the tax rate from 50 percent to 67 percent, by setting a firm maximum on work-related expenses, and by excluding social-security and income taxes as work expenses.

The new medical deduction scheme proposed presented another difficulty. Present recipients with some other income would receive less than the full Medicaid subsidy, while, at the same time, no one would suddenly lose full medical benefits because he earned an additional dollar. The scheme works as follows: one-third of earnings which a family retains above $720 becomes the amount deductible for Medicaid, *i.e.*, the amount of medical costs per year a family must cover before the federal government covers the cost of medical care expenses. Assume a family had a $600 medical bill. Such a family would not be entitled to any subsidized medical care until its earnings equal or exceed $2,520. This scheme leaves present welfare recipients with medical care costs less well off than under the current Medicaid program, where families receive full medical care until their earnings make them ineligible for welfare. Thus, the effort to eliminate the notch problem had the unintended effect of lowering the net economic well-being of families with about average medical care costs.

The efforts to resolve the notch problem within the cost constraints did not transform the welfare system into a work-incentive system. If anything, the new proposals (H.R.1) have even fewer work incentives than the provisions enacted in the 1967 legislation. And many economists would agree with Pechman and Rivlin's testimony that "the most important improvement that could be made would be to lower the marginal tax rate at least to 50 percent."[11] They reach this conclu-

11. Statement on Welfare Reform, Joseph A. Pechman and Alice M. Rivlin, prepared for the Hearings of the Senate Finance Committee, January 21, 1972, mimeo.

sion by taking into account the social-security and income taxes that working welfare recipients would have to pay. These raise the marginal tax rate from 67 percent to 86 percent, which means that the welfare recipient keeps only 14 percent, not 33 percent, from earnings above $720 when the loss in the value of in-kind benefits (such as Medicaid and child-care) are taken into account. Tax rates above 100 percent persist. The administration's efforts to resolve the notch problem have failed.

SUMMARY

I have argued that the primary purpose of welfare reform is to reduce the size and costs of the program, and that the major strategy to achieve this aim was to alter the work behavior of present recipients through a combination of services, economic incentives, and administrative restrictions designed respectively to increase work ability, work incentives, and work requirements. In the long run it was assumed that when services and economic incentives took effect that costs would fall and the size of welfare would decline, even if in the short run both would rise, because the short-run costs were so substantial that reformers recoiled from this assumption.

The service strategy is of doubtful cost-effectiveness when the cost of child-care and training are taken into account. It is also of limited effectiveness, since it seeks to modify skill and motivation without paying attention to the level of unemployment and structure of wages. It operates one-sidedly on the supply of labor, but not the demand for it. Recognition of this anomaly has led to the creation of some jobs in the public sector with the requirement of the assumption that these jobs be held on a temporary basis till permanent employment is located.

The work-incentive approach creates new inequities and prohibitive costs. The use of a lower than 100 percent tax rate for AFDC in 1967 produced embarrassing inequities between the economic situation of those simultaneously on welfare and at work, and the working poor who were not on welfare. A program committed to promoting work incentives could not permit a situation where those at work were worse off than those on welfare. These inequities therefore necessitated inclusion of the working poor under FAP. But lower tax rates both for the working poor and AFDC recipients meant higher costs and a substantially increased welfare population. The administrative response to this problem was to raise the tax rate. At the same time the administration was under pressure to raise the basic guarantee level, since a family of four could not be expected to live on an income of less than half the government-established poverty line. But high tax rates and high guarantees produce work disincentives. Thus the incentive strategy, when combined with the objective of reducing poverty, is self-defeating.

Welfare reform then sought to achieve three aims: to contain the growth of costs and eventually to reduce them; to relieve economic distress by providing a basic guarantee which approached the poverty line; and to promote work-oriented behavior among present welfare recipients. These objectives conflicted. Given the unflagging commitment to transform economically dependent family heads to financial self-sufficiency and thereby to reduce the cost and scope of welfare, and given the ineffectiveness of services and the high cost of economic incentives, it became necessary to place greater reliance upon administrative approaches to get people to work. In addition to federal work-requirements, states broadened their restrictive methods, as many relied on the erosion of the value of welfare payments and increasing the stigma associated with receipt of welfare. The implicit assumption is that rolls will decline as people avoid welfare to preserve their sense of self-dignity. A decline in the case-load for this reason offers testimony that those on welfare could indeed have worked, but chose not to. A restrictive strategy is justified not on the grounds of punishing the poor, but of weeding out ineligibles.

The argument I have set out sees the development of welfare policy during the past decade as a trade-off among these conflicting aims. The incentive strategy is prohibitively costly in both financial and political terms. Since politically the relief of distress as an objective could not be forsaken, and since services during an economic recession have doubtful effects, a restrictive strategy, which always had been accepted, assumed increasing importance.

This interpretation is vulnerable. The legislative history of welfare reform requires a more complicated analysis. It can be argued that it is somewhat arbitrary to isolate three competing objectives and to assign priority to one over-arching purpose. A close reading of the legislative hearing makes it clear that Congress was also concerned with: fiscal relief to the states and cities; raising the incomes of the poorest Southern families and those of the working poor who work full-time, year-round, and are still in economic distress; reducing family break-up, which a system of payments to female heads is presumed to encourage; and decreasing regional migration, which sharp differentials in benefit levels may promote. Even this list of inequities, inadequacies, disincentives, and inefficiencies which needed reform is incomplete. There was also, on the one hand, anxiety about ineligibility as a result of fraud and deception, and, on the other hand, dismay over the discourtesies to which welfare claimants were subjected, and a profound distrust of the size, complexity and cost of the welfare bureaucracy. Which of these multiple aims merit emphasis? The task of sorting out objectives is made more difficult because of the lack of candor in discussions of welfare reform. The emphasis on work-oriented behavior is regarded by at least some individuals in the administration, congress, and those who do the staff work for both, as disingenuous. In private discussions they recognize the difficulties of achieving such an aim, at a low cost and in a short time period, especially during a period of rising unemployment. The insistence of this objective can be better understood as originating from political rather than rational considerations, and therefore to isolate this aim and assign it priority over other purposes is misleading. Finally, the same legislative provision could appeal to quite different constituencies and to very different purposes. Why was it regarded as so crucial to include the working poor? I have argued that this was so because of inequities and the associated work-disincentive effects, but other motives can readily be discerned. It was assumed that a program which excluded male heads might affect family structure, for it promoted an incentive for family break-up. In addition, the working poor were pimarily white and the welfare poor largely black; thus for tactical reasons the acceptability of the program by the public might change if the composition of its recipients was modified. However, if the working poor are included as welfare recipients, there was apprehension that, unless a severe work test was introduced, they might forsake the demeaning work they now accepted in favor of benefits without work. The intrduction of the "no-suitable-work" clause in FAP, which prevents any recipient from rejecting a "suitable" job which was not defined in terms of past labor-force attachment, was a restrictive provision which arose less from anxiety over costs than fear that a "handout" program would threaten the work ethic. Thus, the turning to a more coercive approach can also be interpreted as arising not only from the logical problem which the high costs of low tax rates, adequate grants, and extensive coverage necessitated, but also from the more diffuse public attitudes toward the poor and toward the work ethic.[12]

## The British Experience

The British interest in the reverse income tax, like the American experience, is also inspired by many motives. It does not appear, however, to have been primarily related to a concern for altering work behavior among present Supplementary Beneficiaries (recipients of public assistance) by using income-conditioned benefits as an incentive strategy. Rather, in the British context, a new principle for distributing public funds was sought. It was hoped that tax burdens and total government expenditures could be restrained through increased reliance upon selective policies. Those who could afford to pay more for the use of social services should accept higher user charges, while the poor should selectively receive benefits based on

---

12. I am indebted to Leonard Hausman for calling some of these points to my attention.

a test of income. The underlying rationale is that public benefits should concentrate its scarce resources upon those in greatest need.

This strategy, therefore, called for the gradual reduction of universal and general subsidies. For example, the cost of school meals, which had been subsidized as a part of a broader food subsidy, would be increased. Similarly, in a major pending reform of housing finances, the Conservative government plans to increase rents in public council housing to a level which approaches their market value. Charges in National Health Services programs for prescriptions, dental, and optical costs were also increased. When general subsidies are reduced, prices of school meals, rents, and medical care naturally increase. This produces a strain on the budgets of lower-income families. Therefore, special, means-tested benefits in the form of free school meals, rent rebates, or National Health Service exemptions had to be extended to larger numbers of families to relieve the hardships which accompany the price increases in school meals, rent, and medical care.

In addition to the strategy of reducing general subsidies and relying upon more differentiated means-tests of in-kind programs, the government sought a general cash supplement to aid the working poor, a group that public policy had partially neglected. One of the ways to aid the working poor introduced by the Labour government was by more closely integrating new increases in universally available direct expenditures for family allowances with reduction in the value of tax exemptions for children. This system was known as "claw-back."

FROM CLAW - BACK TO FIS

It may be useful to review briefly how claw-back operated, because the means-tested Family Income Supplements (FIS) bill emerged out of the limits of claw-back. Clawback was introduced in 1968 as a way to selectively concentrate additional benefits in family allowances among the poor. It operated so that the standard rate taxpayer, that is, a family unit who then paid 32 percent of his taxable income on income taxes, received virtually no benefit from these increases—*i.e.*, most of the British tax-paying public. This was accomplished by having the increase in family allowances of 50 pence offset by an equivalent reduction in the total personal tax allowance. In this way, the increase benefited in full those who were below the tax threshold, and also benefited, at least in part, those reduced-rate taxpayers who were paying taxes below the 32 percent level. But since family allowances were subject to income taxes, higher benefits lowered the threshold at which earned income was taxed. The 1968 increase of ℑ 83 million in gross expenditures concentrated only ℑ 47 million on those families paying below the standard tax rate of 32 percent.

By 1970, when the Conservatives took office, the changes that had been introduced in the tax structure virtually eliminated the scope within which the claw-back could concentrate additional resources among the poor. The reduced rates of taxes were abolished (taxes below 32 percent) by Labour in 1969 and 1970 when Labour was still responsible for the budget.[13] At the same time, the value of personal tax allowances was increased, but by an amount which was smaller than that band of income over which the reduced tax rate had been payable. As a result of abolishing the reduced standard tax rate and increasing personal tax allowances, the income level at which the standard rate of tax became payable was lowered. Claw-back also had the effect of creating a double reduction in the tax threshold, because it increased taxable income (family allowances are taxable) and reduced tax allowances, thus further lowering the point at which families start to pay tax. The effect of these tax changes and the net impact of claw-back dramatically limited the further use of claw-back as a means of selectively concentrating further increases in family allowances among the poor. To illustrate the outcome of this process, consider this example: "A man with two children was, in 1970, paying the standard rate of tax with earnings of just over ℑ 16 a week compared with nearly ℑ 20 two years

13. The reduced standard rate of 30 percent on unearned income was eliminated, while earned income was taxed at a higher rate. Later the Conservative government lowered the taxes to 30 percent.

earlier, and yet, under claw-back, neither would benefit from a family allowance increase."[14]

In a period of inflation, wage expansion, and the rapid rise in the value of supplementary benefits which exceeded net average wage levels, British tax policy had inadvertently evolved into a system where the lowest tax bracket, in which the poor are found, is 30 percent. The surtax charge (*i.e.*, taxes at higher rates) did not take effect until earnings had reached ₤ 5,000 per year. The progressive tax system had changed into a proportionate tax for most of the population at a lower tax threshold.

These characteristics of the British tax system had fateful consequences for the further use of claw-back and for the increased reliance upon means-testing. When the Conservatives came into power, these anomalies of the British tax system became evident. Inflation and the general rise in incomes, the decision to treat family allowances as taxable income, and the introduction of claw-back had all contributed to a substantial reduction in the tax threshold. Furthermore, politically the Conservatives found it difficult to ignore the problem of poverty among children. Reform on the Left favors universal programs or, more precisely, benefits which are automatically distributed and which do not isolate the poor as a separate group, subjecting them to differential treatment by virtue of their income status. Specifically, the Child Poverty Action Group supported a tax-free family allowance with substantially higher benefits and the elimination of child tax exemptions to cover part of the costs. However, the government regarded the costs of such a scheme as prohibitive, and initially rejected this route on both financial and political grounds. The only other viable alternative which was being considered was a negative income tax, and, on a small scale, this is essentially the course the Conservative government followed when it developed a family-income-supplements approach to child poverty.

14. David Barker, "The Family Income Supplement," *New Society*, August 5, 1971, p. 241.

In addition to assuring substantial take-up, FIS must avoid work disincentives. Following a brief description of the mechanics of the FIS system, the two problems of take-up and disincentives will be examined.

### THE FAMILY INCOME SUPPLEMENTS PROGRAM

The program is designed for families with children where the head of the family is in full-time work, 30 hours or more per week. To insist on the principle that benefits are paid only to the fully employed departs from most insurance and welfare programs, which typically pay benefits only when work is interrupted. In Britain, since the end of the Speenhamland system of 1795, those in full-time employment were unable to receive welfare benefits (Supplementary Benefits).

The Family Income Supplement scheme is a form of negative income taxation. A "prescribed amount" was fixed for families of different sizes. In August 1971, that amount was set at £18 for a family with one child, with £2 added for each additional child. This established the incme limit above which no benefit is payable. This limit has been raised and will, as of April 1972, begin at £20 per week for a one-child family. Those whose earnings came below this figure had half the difference made up by the state up to a maximum initially set at £3, but later raised to £5 per week, and a minimum of 20 pence. The benefits go only to families where the head is in full-time employment and is therefore ineligible for Supplementary Benefits. Families headed by single parents and couples are treated alike.

Paying benefits to families with "negative net resources" from a prescribed amount which fell below the tax threshold, which also coincided with the poverty line as measured by the value of supplementary benefits, had a compelling logic. But the government decided to raise the prescribed threshold and increase the maximum grant from £4 to £5. These changes had the effect of raising FIS recipients well above the tax threshold. They also had the effect of increasing the size of the eligible population.

The system is nationally administered and designed to sim-
plify the process of eligibility review. Earnings are assessed
on the basis of the five weeks preceding the claim. Once an
award is made, it continues for six months, regardless of any
changes in the composition of the family or any variation in
income during this period. In determining eligibility, the
income of children, capital assets and in-kind benefits can
be taken into account, but at least in the early stages these
sources of income have not been scrutinized. The procedure
for getting a grant has been described by a chief civil servant
as follows:

The claimant:

> must first get a claim form from a post office or a local social security
> office, unless . . . some . . . agency has supplied it unasked. With
> it he gets a franked envelope. He fills in the form, attaches—ideal-
> ly—five weekly pay slips and posts it to Blackpool. (Couples are
> expected to fill in the form together and both are asked to sign.)
> If he has not claimed before and if the family is not drawing family
> allowances [as in the case of a one-child family] he should also
> enclose his children's birth certificates. If he has no pay slips he
> need not wait to send in his claim. In such cases the Department
> of Health and Social Security will send him a form to pass on
> to his employer—all correspondence with employers is conducted
> via the claimant—and if the claim succeeds he will be paid benefits
> from the date of his claim.[15]

A family in receipt of FIS also acquires a passport which
entitles him to other means-tested benefits such as free prescription charges, free dental services, free school meals, etc.

PROBLEMS OF TAKE-UP AND WORK DISINCENTIVES

In the British debate the Family Income Supplement faces
two problems: take-up and work disincentives. We briefly consider each problem, the kinds of administrative action taken
to reduce them, and the new problems and opportunities
created by these efforts. Whereas American public policy

15. John Stackpoole, "Running FIS," *New Society*, Jan. 13, 1972, p. 65.

seems almost obsessed with the problem of how to reduce the size of the welfare case-load, by contrast British policy is preoccupied with how to reach the universe of eligible recipients.

*The problem of take-up.* A serious indictment of a means-tested program designed to augment the income of the poor is that it fails to reach those for whom it was designed. Most critics of FIS have argued that there is something inherent which generates low take-up in individualized means-testing where an applicant must apply for benefits. These critics have argued that at best a means-tested program is able to reach only two-thirds of those for whom it is intended, and it seems likely that the remaining group might include those who were in greatest need. The criticism is taken seriously. The Secretary of State for Health and Social Services affirmed the objective that the program should reach at least 85 percent of its eligible population, or an estimated 140,000 claimants of working families. This declaration made the issue of take-up a sensitive political concern. The success of the program seemed to depend upon the government's ability to reach the goal of 85 percent participation.

What then can be said about the experience? At the early stages, the take-up was discouragingly low. Between May 3 and June 22, 1971, there were only 12,284 successful claims. With a revised estimate of about 140,000 working families and 25,000 wage-stopped families as the potential universe of eligible beneficiaries, the results were discouraging. The Prime Minister himself became involved in the issue of low take-up, and civil servants were informed that the campaign must not fail. ₤60,000 had already been spent during the first weeks of the campaign to publicize FIS. With backing from the Prime Minister, an additional quarter of a million pounds was available to be spent in the weeks before the program became operational on August 3. By December 1971, ₤310,000 had been spent on the campaign, an amount equal to about 5 percent of total money payments for Supplementary Benefits.

By the end of 1971, there were only 93,000 recipients, a number still well short of the revised estimate of 165,000 families eligible for benefits.[16] Take-up varied with the value of the benefits. The average weekly payment was ƺ 1.72. Approximately 75 percent of eligible families with claims of ƺ 2 or more per week take up their benefits. The government claimed that the large majority of those who failed to apply were the marginal cases who could hope to receive only a small amount.

Why did so few families come forward in the early stages of the campaign? Several speculations can be advanced. It is always difficult to make the public aware of a new product. Cigarette commercials spend substantially more on advertising a new product, and it seems unreasonable to expect quick results. After all, low-income families will learn about these benefits essentially through word of mouth. If individuals judge the value of benefits to be substantial and relatively easy to secure without a sense of stigma associated with the process of application, then over time this informal system will take hold and applications will rise. Of course, quite different interpretations might be placed upon the eligibility process as seen by the clients themselves. For example, both the husband and wife have to sign the form and declare their income. In a period of wage inflation, husbands may not have informed their wives about the salary increases they acquired, and hence may be reluctant to do so now if the value of the benefits they are to receive are only modest.

A second interpretation is that low take-up is largely an artifact based on a mis-estimate of the universe of eligibles. Government statisticians over-estimated the number of families with eligible children at work full time and living below the supplementary benefit line. A period of rapid wage inflation contributed even further to the erosion in the size of the eligible group. Many low-income families hold several jobs and enjoy overtime and would thus disqualify for benefits.

16. House of Commons Hansard, Oral Answers, Dec. 21, 1971, Vol. 828, col. 1293 - 94.

Estimates of moonlighting and overtime were not readily available. Moreover, in an era where most people pay income taxes, it is to be expected there would be tax dodging at the lower-income as well as the more subtle forms of tax evasion at the upper-income level. For those at the low-income level, application for means-tested benefits might be construed as a trap that would lead to a discovery of their tax evasions. Of course, those who are unemployed could apply for supplementary benefits instead of FIS. Thus, one-third of the beneficiaries of FIS are female-headed households who work full time. According to this interpretation FIS will fizzle, a victim of miscalculation.

Alternatively, the low take-up figures may suggest that there are intrinsic limitations of income-tested programs which are not automatically distributed but require special applications. According to this argument, even the most efficient means-tested program will reach about two-thirds of its eligible population. The low take-up figures can be interpreted as evidence of the failure of a non-automatic selective system where recipients must apply for grants as a general strategy for improving the economic well-being of the low-wage sector.

The evaluation of take-up in means-tested programs is bedeviled by technical problems—there is no firm way of knowing the universe of eligible persons. Thus the debate remains inconclusive. It is worth noting, however, that a slight increase in the limits of income eligibility significantly alters the universe of eligibles; it also follows that, in a period of inflation, failure to pay attention to maintaining the income levels of eligibility must lead to the gradual decline in the number of eligibles. This suggests that means-testing may be an acceptable form of distribution when public attention is riveted on it as a critical issue of the day. As attention shifts to other areas of public concern, the level of eligibility may drift downward and the universe of eligibles automatically decrease. An assessment of the merits of means-testing must also take account of these political factors of administration.

Still the government remained anxious about the take-up

level. Undoubtedly it was concerned about the size of the eligible group and the level of benefits. Shortly after the program was in effect, it was decided to raise the prescribed amount and to increase the maximum grant. This expanded the number of eligibilities and raised the value of the grant. Under the new regulations, the earning limit for a family with three children would be ℥ 24. Such a family with total income of ℥ 16 could therefore receive a payment of ℥ 4 per week. This is a substantial amount, since it is equal to 25 percent of the family's original income.

But, as we have pointed out, the move to reduce the take-up problem created a new anomaly. Many families cross the tax threshold before they stop receiving FIS payments. Thus the government was giving benefits on the one hand and extracting taxes on the other hand, creating for these families an effective tax rate on the increase of new earning of 85 percent—3 percent from income taxes, approximately 5 percent for National Insurance contributions, 50 percent from FIS.

In the Chancellor's budget speech of March 1972, the tax threshold was raised by increasing the personal tax allowance for the single person and married couple. A family man with two children started paying taxes when his income reached ℥ 18.79 a week. As a result of the increase in the child tax allowance and the proposed increase in the married allowance, after April 1972 this family will not start to pay taxes until his earned income reaches ℥ 21.50.[17]

The Conservative government was concerned with reducing general subsidies, expanding the well-being of the working poor, and substituting a new principle of public finance which would reduce tax burdens by distributing public expenditures more selectively. It was therefore politically important to resolve this central dilemma of means-testing—its failure to reach those for whom it was designed. To address the take-up problem in FIS, three main approaches were tried: widespread and costly publicity, centralized and simplified administration, and increases in the level of benefits and the threshold of

17. *Financial Times*, March 22, 1972, excerpt from a chancellor's speech.

eligibility. General subsidies were in the meantime successively withdrawn from food, housing, and medical care, thus extending means-testing well beyond the poverty level and reaching deeply into the income structure. Without having resolved the problem of take-up, the very effort to do so by making benefits more attractive exacerbated yet another problem, that of tax inequities, as those judged in need of benefits were subjected to income tax. It also made more visible the potential work disincentives which arise when the poor and near-poor pay income and social-security taxes as well as high implicit marginal taxes which lead to "the poverty trap"— over 100 percent marginal tax rate.

THE PROBLEM OF WORK DISINCENTIVES: NOTCHES
AND THE HIGH RATE OF TAXATION

The new income limits for FIS and other means-tested programs are well above the point at which many families start paying income tax. An overlap between the positive-taxation system and the social-benefits systems emerged. After April 1972 the tax threshold for a family with three children is just under ℈ 21. When a family begins to pay taxes, it is faced with an initial marginal tax rate of 30 percent on its additional earnings. Moreover, the benefit from certain means-tested programs falls or vanishes entirely as incomes rise above the tax threshold. As the income of a family with three children rises from ℈ 21 to 24 per week (three-quarters of average male industrial earnings), it passes through bands of income within which the sum of the new tax liabilities and foregone benefits exceeds increased income. This is the "notch" problem. It produces the anomaly, discussed in more detail below, of re-ordering the rankings of families after FIS, other means-tested benefits, and taxes are taken into account. A less extreme and more general difficulty is posed by the very high rate at which families are taxed as earnings increase. Tony Lynes, the first full-time secretary of the Child Poverty Action Group, demonstrates the effect of taxes and selected lost benefits on families with income below average earnings in the city of Birmingham, which had already put into effect an extensive rebate scheme.

As a family increases its earnings from ℨ 13 to ℨ 14, total money income rises by only 28 pence. Thus, 72 percent of the increase has been "taxed" away by the combination of taxes paid out and benefits lost. Each subsequent ℨ 1 of increase in earnings are taxed at rates of 73, 73, 84, 84, 184, 121 percent. (A notch occurs when the percentage exceeds 100 percent.) The high tax rate in Birmingham is in part due to the structure of the new rent-rebate scheme. Tenants are eligible for rebates within a narrow income range, and benefits are therefore withdrawn rapidly as income increases.[18]

The rate at which several benefits are lost and increased taxes paid, *i.e.*, the cumulative marginal tax rate, is presumed to affect the work behavior of those who might consider working harder or longer to obtain higher pay. Of course, the government has been aware of the presumed work-incentives problem that means-testing presents. Efforts have been made to lower the marginal tax in several ways: a low 17 percent rate for new means-tests like rent rebates; staggering the income cut-off points among different existing programs;[19] raising the tax threshold, by raising the child tax allowance and personal tax allowance for single people and married couples; and making families above the tax threshold ineligible for means-tested programs. Such solutions are taken in isolation. It is politically difficult to achieve integrated decisions.

*Impact of work disincentives*: How serious in reality are the work disincentive effects of the high tax rates? The answer must depend on how many families receive more than one means-tested program, whether families know about the level of the cumulative marginal tax, and whether this knowledge affects their work behavior. Little is known about each of these

18. Tony Lynes, "Family Income Super Tax," *New Society*, May 6, 1971 and David Barker, "The Family Income Supplement," *New Society*, August 5, 1971.

19. Consider the case of staggering benefits. There appears to be pressure among several specialized bureaucracies to raise the cut-off points and to widen the eligibility to middle-income groups. Thus the staggering of the cut-off points may be a logical solution to notches and high cumulative tax rates but politically difficult to achieve.

questions. Only a *prima facie* argument can therefore be developed. It is, however, widely presumed that if access to multiple means-tested programs was widespread and if people were economically worse off from an increase in earnings (notch), or no better off (high marginal tax rates), they would act rationally, choosing benefits over wage increases. In effect, they would, if free to choose, select that level of earnings which maximizes total money income (after taxes and benefits).

This general argument has been advanced by those on Child Poverty Action Group (CPAG), at the political Left and the Institute of Economic Affairs on the political Right. The Left has not hesitated to advance the position that marginal tax rates create work disincentives as part of their broader attack on means-tested programs. For example, Michael Meacher, Labour backbencher, criticized the government White Paper which proposed a national rent rebate scheme to provide an income-conditioned housing allowance, on the grounds that it has inherent disincentive effects. He argued that "if the Tories are right, and incentives matter, how can they justify measures that sharply reduce the incentives for the poor to work harder and earn more?" A *Times* report observes, "It is . . . quaint to find the radical Left complaining of state aid draining the poor of an incentive to help themselves."[20] It seems doubtful that the CPAG is seriously exercised about the possibilities that work behavior might be altered. But the trade unions are anxious, in view of the possible effect on wage claims. The unions now recognize the effect higher benefits have on augmenting the marginal tax rates, and oppose these rates on grounds of equity as well. On the other hand, it may be argued that the average worker in Britain works long hours, and if these social benefits could achieve for him the same net income while decreasing his working hours, over-all utility should be improved. Shorter hours might also reduce the rising levels of unemployment, so that over-all productivity would not decline. When a worker has an opportunity to change

20. Nigel Lawson, "An Achilles Heel About the Poor," *The Times*, July 29, 1971.

his occupational status, rather than the number of hours
worked, then we expect that he would prefer the better job,
since it offers status, improved working conditions, and other
non-economic factors which accompany upward mobility, even
if high marginal tax rates leave him with no added earning
power. Moreover, continued eligibility for FIS depends on
meeting the work test of continued full time employment
(defined as 30 hours per week). FIS benefits create a positive
incentive for a family head to continue to work. Under the
new regulations, FIS can augment earnings for a three-child
family earning at ₹16 by as much as 25 percent. The head
of such a family may have an economic motive for working
less, but not for quitting work altogether. In other ways FIS
is neutral with respect to work-oriented behavior. The wage-
stop rule under the Supplementary Benefits program requires
that benefits from welfare not exceed potential income when
earning. Benefits from FIS are added to income when earning
whether or not they were acquired. Thus the working poor
receive the value of FIS whether they are at work or on welfare.
This procedure also reduces the number of wage-stopped
families.

Aside from the FIS work requirements, there are other
administrative devices in the established procedures of the
Supplementary Benefits Commission for discouraging
involuntary employment and encouraging or coercing those
on welfare to seek work. For example, if it is felt by the Supplementary Benefits Commission that a man has left his job
without a good reason, the Commission is required to disallow
part of his benefit for six weeks. With growing unemployment,
use of this procedure has increased. In addition, the unemployed on welfare are required to register weekly as available
for work, subjected to the wage stop, interviewed periodically
by employment counsellors to determine the reasons for their
failure to work, and can be sent to jail for failing to maintain
themselves or their dependents. In 1968, new approaches were
introduced by the Labour government. The four-week and
three-month rules are an example of such new procedures
of the Supplementary Benefits Commission for discouraging

the work-shy. These rules operate as follows. Unskilled, physically and mentally fit single men under age 45, living in areas with low rates of unemployment are advised when they receive benefits that if they do not secure work at the end of four weeks they will have to reapply. Skilled men and those with dependents are given a three-month warning. If a man renews his request, the Supplementary Benefits Commission will review his efforts to get work as part of a procedure for rewarding benefits. It is incumbent upon the claimant to prove that he has met the "genuinely seeking work" requirements.

While it is in principle possible for low-skilled workers with large families to be as well-off on welfare as in full-time employment, stringent administrative devices are in effect to encourage the work-shy to work. These administrative rules were, however, in effect long before the introduction of FIS. We cannot therefore conclude that the negative income tax for those in full time employment contributed to and increased reliance upon restrictive approaches to prevent work disincentives. The motives which inspired the introduction of these restrictive rules in Supplementary Benefits are varied and it is not necessary to view all work tests as punitive. Considerations of equity have apparently played some role in the introduction of the four-week and three-month rules under the Labor government.[21] These rules also suggest a trade-off between restriction and adequacy, defined as a narrow gap between net earnings and maximum benefits.

In summary, it is difficult to assess the impact of the cumulative addition of various tax rates from income and social benefits on the incentive of low-wage earners to make a

21. Prior to the introduction of the four-week and three-month rules in 1968, local employment review officers were given discretion to determine at what point a man must declare himself available to accept work which departs from his usual and customary job. After this time a man must accept whatever job is available. Thus, the timing of when to exert pressure on a man to lower his sights for work was inequitably administered. Richard Titmuss asserts that the motive for introducing these new rules was equity, *i.e.*, to replace arbitrary discretion with an administrative rule. For example, 300 young men in Kensington (a middle-class residential area) applied for work as mass-media visual activator (TV work). These middle-class youths were treated more leniently than their working-class counterparts.

sustained efort to increase their own earnings. There is little evidence about how widespread is the multiple usage of services, the linkage between knowledge of high taxation on actual work behavior is uncertain, and the effectiveness of established work-test policies to discourage workers from dropping out of the labor force is untested. Perhaps uncertainty leads to cautious policies. While the severity of the problem of work disincentives is unsettled, it does appear clear that even hypothetical high taxes and notches offend public policy on grounds of equity, regardless of the actual impact such procedures have on work behavior.

The inequity arises because of the efforts to aid the poor through a multiplicity of means-tested programs lead, as critics have caustically noted, to paying surtaxes while being on the dole. The irony of this policy is made more vivid since the government has lowered marginal tax rates for the top income tax brackets from 91 to 75 percent as a means of revitalizing the economy through incentives. Perversely, positive incentives for high-income groups yield lower tax rates, whereas improvements in the economic position of the poor produces even higher tax rates than the rich are expected to pay. The inequity surrenders to a glaring anomaly for the small number of families who cross the positive tax threshold before they stop receiving FIS. Even before any other means tests are considered, the effective tax rate on the marginal pound is 85 percent (a marginal income tax of 30 percent, National Insurance taxes of 5 percent and a marginal tax on FIS of 50 percent). For the poor, adequate social income and work incentives conflict, whereas, at least in principle, for the well-to-do they reinforce each other.

INCOME EQUALIZATION AND RADICAL REFORM

Even so perverse a system is not without its compensating features. An uncoordinated, fragmented, means-tested benefit system with high tax rates may contribute powerfully to the attainment of redistributive aims, which is a goal shared by both those who favor selective and those who prefer universal welfare programs. The debate about the high tax rate and work-incentives has obscured this point. Some observers have reluctantly noted that "from an extreme egalitarian point of view, there may be something to be said for this situation."[22]

The present system in Britain does appear to contribute to some income-equalization among those earning less than national average earnings, if we assume that at each income-level families do indeed take advantage of the social benefits of rebates on rent and on rates (property taxes) and Family Income Supplements to which they are entitled. These means tests, combined with positive taxes, can augment by as much as one-fourth the earnings of families in the low-wage sector (earnings between ʒ13 and ʒ17), while they can take away between one and 30 percent of the earnings of those in the ʒ18—ʒ22 income band. This produces a pattern of income equalization between those with low wages and those at three-quarters of average wages, compressing the total income spread of the bottom and the near middle workers. Such a system contributes nothing to equalizing the income of the top- and the middle-income earners. The distribution of earning is squeezed at the lower end while it is stretched at the upper end.

Table 7.1 sets out the evidence for families with two children (ages four and six) in the city of Birmingham in 1971 on which these conclusions are based. The data show that, for earnings between ʒ13 and ʒ23 per week, the dispersion of total net money income narrows dramatically, once benefits and taxes are taken into account.

On the assumption of high take-up of all social benefits, not only have incomes been equalized, but the initial rank-ordering of families has been altered. And this falling out of the income queue arises largely because of the effects of the degressive tax system, combined with an overlap between the system of collecting taxes and dispersing benefits. The income cut-off points for some means-tested programs reach far beyond the point at which individuals are expected to start paying

22. Tony Lynes, *New Society*, May 6, 1971. David Donnison, Director of the Center for Environmental Studies has in conversation noted the same point.

TABLE 7.1. *Social Benefits, Taxation, and Income Equalization* [a]

| 1 | 2 | 3 | 4 | 5 | 6 | 7 |
|---|---|---|---|---|---|---|
| | | Other | Earnings | | | |
| | | Social | plus | National | Income | Total |
| Weekly Earnings | Family Allowance | Benefits [b] | Benefits | Insurance | Tax | Income |
| | | | (1+2+3) | = | | (4-5-6) |
| 13 | .90 | 6.52 | 20.42 | 1.08 | | 19.34 |
| 14 | .90 | 5.85 | 20.75 | 1.13 | | 19.62 |
| 15 | .90 | 5.16 | 21.06 | 1.18 | | 19.88 |
| 16 | .90 | 4.48 | 21.38 | 1.22 | | 20.16 |
| 17 | .90 | 3.79 | 21.69 | 1.27 | | 20.42 |
| 18 | .90 | 2.96 | 21.86 | 1.33 | .23 | 20.30 |
| 19 | .90 | 2.09 | 21.99 | 1.37 | .53 | 20.09 |
| 20 | .90 | 1.42 | 22.32 | 1.42 | .83 | 20.07 |
| 21 | .90 | 0.75 | 22.65 | 1.46 | 1.13 | 20.06 |
| 22 | .90 | | 22.90 | 1.50 | 1.43 | 19.97 |
| 23 | .90 | | 23.90 | 1.55 | 1.73 | 20.62 |

a. Adapted from a table of Birmingham families with 2 children, ages 4 and 6, Tony Lynes, "Family Income Super Tax," *New Society*, May 6, 1971.

b. FIS, rent allowance and rate rebate.

progressive taxation. Thus, the government is extending to families social benefits based on the criterion of need, while at the same time taxing their income.

These inequities and anomalies arise from the existence of two parallel systems: "a taxation system which embodies a set of reliefs and allowances based on one set of principles, and a social security system which embodies a different set of benefits and allowances based on a different set of principles." Although Richard Titmuss had almost two decades ago criticized the inequities which arise from this form of dualism, the above quote comes not from disciples of Titmuss or the political Left, but from the Conservative Chancellor of the Exchequer in his 1972 Budget Speech. And his proposal for reform is as far-reaching as is his assessment of the problem. He proposed a scheme which would provide a single assessment of income to be taxed at a 30 percent marginal rate, and which would, therefore, serve for calculating both the outstanding taxes above a specific tax threshold and the social benefits to be paid out for those with income below that level. Here is a negative income tax, integrated with the tax system. Clearly, the scheme was defined in more positive terms as a system of credits. Some of the details of the scheme were presented in the Budget Message.

All forms of personal tax allowances—single, married, and child allowances—would disappear, and many forms of social benefits would also be abolished, including family allowances with claw-back and the family income supplement. Even so, a broad spectrum of the means-tested programs would remain unintegrated into the new scheme, including free school meals, exemption from health services charges, and rent and rate rebates. Credits would be extended whether or not the recipient was a taxpayer, since they would be "set off against tax payable but where the credit was greater than the tax the difference would be paid as an addition to the wage or other income." The scheme would be universal, because the value of the benefits would remain constant as incomes rose; and the benefit would be provided automatically without an individual means test. These credits against taxes would continue to be paid during periods of illness and unemployment. In other words, all those eligible would get a flat rate credit to be set off against income tax. Those who pay taxes would treat the credit as income exempted from taxation, while those whose income was lower than the credit amount would receive it in the form of transfers.

As *The Economist* points out,[23] the credit proposal will divide the critics of the government's social policy. But the crucial question now will be how selective the credit system will be. The new tax threshold will be set by the value of the basic credits, which presumably could not be lower than

23."Giving Credit," *The Economist*, March 25, 1972, p. 14. Full details of the scheme will be published in a Green Paper (a paper intended for public debate rather than immediate parliamentary action) and a bipartisan select committee will be formed to study the proposal and submit a report.

the existing personal and child allowances combined with value of family allowances. To replace FIS it will need to be higher. But the combined value of these benefits is much lower than the Supplementary Benefit scale rates. Even if the maximum FIS payment were included, the benefits would fall short of the established poverty line. A 30 percent negative tax rate must lead either to a low basic allowance or to a very high break-even point. The new tax threshold will have to be very high if the credit system is to be as generous as the present welfare system is for people with low incomes. Such a system will be costly. What specific proposals the Conservative government will make, and how this dilemma will be resolved in the end, must await future developments.

## Summary and Conclusion

Social policy in the U.S. and Britain has made use of the principle that benefits vary inversely with income, such that as incomes rise there is some proportionate decline in the benefits received. This principle has been extended to the working poor in Britain (FIS) and to welfare recipients in the United States; new legislation proposes its further extension to the working poor (H.R.1). Neither country has yet introduced a true negative income tax, where transfers are conditioned *only* by income and closely integrated into the positive tax structure. Where the principle has been used, benefits are behavior-conditioned, *i.e.*, welfare recipients must register for suitable work in the United States, or already hold a full time job in Britain. The only feature of a negative tax which has been accepted is that some proportion of benefits is retained as earnings rise. The proposed tax credit system in Britain would, if implemented, become the most extensive application of the principle of negative taxation ever carried out by any country. When projected on a large scale and integrated with the positive tax system, it is a far-reaching and basic reform.

If the essence of the NIT is that benefits are income- and not work-conditioned, then it also follows that all forms of income could be subject to the same tax arrangements, not simply income from earnings. Non-employment income from social security or family allowances would also have to be taxed. There would need to be a more integrated and logical ordering of all benefits and taxes, including income and social-security taxes, and the whole system of means-tested social benefits. The 1972 tax credit reform proposed in Britain is such a comprehensive reform. But even so, most means-tested programs would be retained.

Welfare-reform proposals in the United States have not projected so encompassing a reform. Because the present income tax system is taken as the basic constraint, the pure negative-income-tax approach (which relates all forms of income to benefits) is subject to a dilemma from which it cannot escape. If the marginal tax rate is to be kept sufficiently low so as to avoid glaring work disincentives, the poverty level or basic allowance level must also be kept low. But if allowances are set at or near the poverty levels (a level presently enjoyed by welfare recipients residing in high-benefit states, where nearly two-thirds of all present recipients reside), high marginal tax rates are inescapable, if cost constraints are accepted as politically necessary. Thus the hope that economic incentives alone could encourage work is illusory.

Most surprisingly, therefore, when we consider present policy we find that both countries have accepted a work test as a condition for eligibility: in the U.S., work registration; in Britain, full time employment. While accepting the many purposes of welfare reform, I believe that Congress primarily viewed the negative income tax as one approach to alter the work behavior of present welfare recipients. By contrast, FIS in Britain appears to be more preoccupied with supplementing the income of the working poor, and its rules of eligibility are neutral with respect to augmenting work behavior. The purposes of policy are more crucial than its form. I have argued that in the American context the use of the incentive principle leads to restriction, whereas in the British context it contributes to income equalization, at least at the lower end of the earning spectrum, and to proposals for radical tax reform. The argument may be briefly recapitulated as follows.

In the United States it was politically unacceptable to have a low, minimum basic allowance level. In 1969, the President proposed $1,600 for a family of four under the FAP. In H.R.1, a $2,400 poverty level was set by cashing out the $800 value of food stamps. Such a scheme seemed to offer both fiscal relief to the states through federal take-over of welfare costs, and a visible step in the direction of reducing poverty. But at this high guarantee level it was not thought possible to retain the 50 percent marginal tax rate which FAP initially proposed. The arithmetic of negative taxation is the villain. The original FAP plan yielded a break-even point of $3,920 (a $1,600 guarantee, a 50 percent tax, and a $720 work expenses disregard). Under this scheme, 14 percent of all families would be covered by FAP. Raising the guarantee by $800 and keeping the same level of disregards and tax rates increases the break-even point to $5,520 and covers 22.4 percent of all American families. A 50 percent increase in the value of the basic allowance triples the costs of the original proposal and expands the eligible population by 57 percent. Given both the cost constraint and the self-evident political difficulty of proposing a reform which would place nearly one American in four on welfare, it seemed necessary to raise the marginal tax to 67 percent. The dilemma is illustrated with Senator Ribicoff's proposal which calls for an even more generous minimum benefit of $3,000 to be gradually raised to the poverty line, a lower tax rate of 60 percent, full payment of income and social-security taxes and work-related expenses as incurred, and which allows for raising the basic allowance to take account of inflation. As Senator Curtis observed, such a scheme would by 1977 place one-third of the population on some welfare benefits.

Welfare reform tried to avoid the Curtis dilemma. In the efforts to save money, H.R.1 not only lowered the proportion of benefits retained as earnings were raised but, like the British, did not reimburse welfare recipients for the taxes they paid. Consequently, as soon as a family's income passes the threshold for paying taxes, additional earnings are reduced at a rate of 86.2 percent. There is no smooth gradation from the area of receiving benefits to that of paying taxes, and the family falls victim to the poverty surtax. Even this high marginal tax rate excludes from consideration the implicit loss of income a family suffers when rising earnings induce ineligibility for other means-tested goods and services, especially Medicaid, but including as well public housing for the more limited group which receives them. For these reasons, the incentive power of the negative income tax has limited scope. Because congressional policy assigns high priority to the aim of reducing AFDC rolls and costs—or, at least, abating their rise—failure of the incentive system has led to increased reliance upon administrative devices which oblige recipients to work. This means more coercion. The demand by liberal economists for a lower negative income tax rate as the single most important and urgently needed change in H.R.1 is therefore politically naive.

In the British context, the policies surrounding negative taxation have evolved into radical proposals for tax and social-service reform. FIS recipients who pay taxes are subject to about the same marginal tax rates with each additional pound of earning as are welfare recipients in the United States. This arises because the positive tax rate is not graded, but starts at 30 percent, while the FIS rate is 50 percent and National Insurance taxes stand at about 5 percent. Thus a tax-paying FIS recipient is subject to an 85 percent tax rate before taking account of the marginal tax on other benefits.

These high tax rates do not apply to all families, but only certain families in particular income bands and of specific compositions who are eligible for specific types of benefits. A partial response to this difficulty has been to stagger the cut-off points of means-tested programs such as FIS, rent and rate rebates, school meals, prescription charges, and other means-tested programs. This has proved difficult to do politically, and, instead, all break-even points have been raised. This forces the means-tested system to reach upward into and above the median wage structure. But this has produced an anomaly, since these higher means-tested limits are well above the point at which many families start paying income tax. The tax threshold was raised substantially in April 1972 to avoid subjecting families who are believed to be in need to an income tax. But the Conservative government has gone still further in its proposal for a major redefinition of the borderline between taxation and social benefits. A new system of tax credits was proposed, representing the most radical reform of social policy in Britain for a quarter of a century.

The need for a bold new approach arises in part from the already widespread use of means-testing, its accelerated expansion, and the special problems of equity, incentives, and take-up which such programs inherently present. In 1967, a conservative estimate placed 20—25 percent of all families in Britain as potentially eligible for one or another means-tested benefits.[24] But since that date, a new means-test (FIS) has been introduced, the cut-off point for established programs such as school dinners and rate rebates has been substantially increased, and the new Fair Deal for Housing will substantially increase the number of households eligible for this new nationally administered housing allowance. The number of persons eligible for means-tested benefits has accordingly expanded greatly. High cumulative tax levels which means-testing requires pose awkward anomalies, even as they augment the net income of low-wage workers and contribute to income equalization between the bottom- and the middle-wage earner while inequalities between the middle and the top grow wider. Such a policy may raise a question about whether these benefits are a substitute for higher wages (as in the case of family allowances in France); however, since the benefits are not paid directly by employer taxes but from general taxes, this question of the substitution of benefits for wages may be avoided. The unions are more troubled by the high marginal taxes than these equity issues. Still, when redistribution is encouraged on the governmental-expenditure side through transfers, rather than from earned income, the issue cannot long be overlooked.

24. A. R. Prest, *Social Benefits and Tax Rates*, London, The Institute of Economic Affairs, 1970, p. 20.

Means-testing in Britain has led to a political debate about the limits of income-conditioned benefits. It has taken the form of an expensive campaign to assure that benefits reach the group for which they were intended. The politics of take-up contrasts sharply with American concern for cutbacks in welfare. And this reflects the different objectives which welfare reform hopes to achieve in each country. To solve the take-up problem, the Conservative government has provided higher benefits and raised the cut-off point for eligibility. But in addressing one problem, yet another is created. Taxes and benefits overlapped and high marginal tax rates followed. Government seems unable to stagger the cut-off points which contribute to these high marginal tax rates, but it has been more successful in raising the tax threshold. While the implicit problems of work incentives which uncoordinated means-testing raises have not been resolved, it is difficult to assess their importance. It seems unlikely that these rates will create work disincentives which lead families to stop working, although it may lead some to work less. Still, the poverty surtax which the cumulation of means tests presents is an embarrassment, on grounds of equity rather than incentives. This has led to higher tax thresholds created by more generous tax exemptions for children and personal tax allowances, and to a proposal for a radical integration of services and taxes by a system of tax credits.

Are there any lessons to be learned from this comparative review of the development of two systems of negative income tax policy serving dramatically different purposes?

The task of drawing lessons from patterns is fraught with much danger. If policies cannot be understood in isolation from the political, cultural, and economic context in which they arise, then comparative studies have limited value in transferring ideas from one country to another. If policy develops, at least in a fair measure, by accident and by administrative considerations, then the scope for studying patterns in order to infer lessons has more promise. I proceed on this latter assumption. Perhaps the most striking conclusion to be

reached for this comparative review is that each system has
its limitations; each new intervention creates new problems
which need to be resolved. There are no final solutions.
Secondly, the same principles, when applied to different purposes, yield different outcomes. It is not the negative income
tax principle itself which leads to restriction, but the purposes
to which the principle is applied. When it is used simultaneously to relieve distress and to alter work behavior, as in the
United States, costs of constraints encourage the expanded
use of restrictive policies. In Britain, the same principle
applied to the aim of expanding consumption of the working
poor posed two problems—take-up and incentives. The solution of the take-up problem by raising benefits and expanding
eligibles exacerbated the problem of incentives by creating
overlap between the tax and benefit system. Some income-
equalization emerged as take-up expanded. However, the
program altered the rank-ordering of families in the income
distribution. In this way, inequities arising from the poverty
surtax became evident. While the political acceptability of
means tests may be increased when they reach middle-income
groups, the inequities and anomalies of means-testing cannot
be avoided. A fragmented and uncoordinated program which
increases the aggregate expenditures available to families cannot resolve these dilemmas. Radical proposals seem necessary,
and a major restructuring of the tax and social benefit system
seems urgently needed as a response to these dilemmas. But
if the most glaring anomalies of poverty surtaxes are eliminated
by raising the tax thresholds and integrating the tax and
benefits system, yet a new dilemma must shortly emerge. A
generous credit system which could significantly reduce the
size and cost of the Supplementary Benefits program must
precipitously raise the tax threshold, and such a scheme will
be as costly as it is redistributive. Tax credits would cost about
₤ 1.3 billion and would reduce by one-third the numbers drawing Supplementary Benefits. In a period of inflation, when
government recognizes in taxes an amount proportionately
higher than its increased expenditures, such higher outlays

may be paid for by fiscal drag. But the pressure for tax reduction, especially in periods of rising unemployment, as a means to stimulate the economy, are difficult to resist. Hence the program may be financed by regressive taxes, such as the value added tax. But the fate of the tax credit system is uncertain. It seems certain that compromises will emerge, and these will create new inequities as policy continues to evolve from one set of contradictions to another.

# V

# Conclusion

S. M. Miller *is Professor of Urban Studies (Sociology and Education) at New York University. He holds a B.A. from Brooklyn College, and an M.A. in economics from Columbia. From Princeton he received both an M.A. in economics and sociology, and the Ph.D. in sociology. Before coming to N.Y.U. he taught at Rutgers University, Brooklyn College, and Syracuse University. Dr. Miller has published extensively on topics of credentialism, working class and lower class life styles, poverty, inequality, and social mobility. The central theme of his work has been inequality, redistribution and social stratification, and his methodology is a combination of social and economic analysis. He is currently working on trends in the distribution of income and other resources in capitalist and socialist nations. His most recent book (with Pamela Roby) is* The Future of Inequality.

# 8

# On Not Abusing Incentives

S. M. MILLER

"The abuse of a thing is not an
argument against its correct use."

Incentives is another tool that has appeared as economists
have moved from business to the world of government. Earlier
tools provided and heralded by economists have been cost-
benefit analysis and PPBS (Planning-Program-Budget-Sys-
tem). As Bruno Stein has pointed out in the opening chap-
ter, incentives are a procedure which can have enormous
impact upon improving the practice of government.

Incentives are intended to achieve the rationalizing of
American policy formation and operation. The objective is to
pull together policies so that they operate in the directions
intended, and to construct policies which will produce desired
results. A simple behavioristic model of how to obtain change
is involved. To a large extent many, if not most, government
policies are efforts to obtain desired behaviors on the part
of business and consumers by punishing them. If they violate
a government regulation, then they are punished. The effort
to avoid punishment leads to the kind of behavior which is
desired. In incentive approaches, the coin is turned over. The
emphasis is now upon the reward side of the punishment-
reward continuum. (It is important to realize that incentives
are part of a continuum, and that various mixes of punishment
and rewards are developed.) The hope is to harness the motivations of businessmen and consumers—the private actors of

199

the American economy—to the ends desired by government policy-makers. The means is to provide monetary benefits to those who behave in desired ways.

Incentives should not connote only rewards for approved behaviors. Financial penalties can be exacted for undesired behaviors. An example of approval rewards is Nixon's "New Economic Policy" of providing tax gains for businesses which buy U.S. rather than foreign goods. A punitive *disincentive* would be taxes on firms which pollute rivers, rather than a compulsory policy which bars such behavior. Incentives imply disincentives, and compulsions may eventually be the most effective policy.

The other drive toward incentives is to recognize that a number of existing practices are dysfunctional. Existing incentives motivate people frequently to move in directions which are counter to objectives. Consequently, the turn toward incentives is a way of trying to make sure that the incentives affecting individuals and firms motivate them in desirable rather than undesirable or counter-productive directions. Getting rid of disincentives is a crucial aspect of utilizing incentives.

Thus one can see the incentive orientation as a way of adapting business approaches to government: businesses and people will do what they are rewarded to do. In a sense, the incentive orientation intends to marry the market to public policy, to adapt the market-place influence to reward the effective carrying out of public policy objectives. This occurs, paradoxically, when there is increasing doubt about the effectiveness·of the American market as an allocator of resources and an efficient mechanism for responding to changes in consumer demand. (Interestingly, the movement from command practices to motivational-incentive practices in socialist countries is probably the best advertising for a market orientation.)

There is a danger of *overselling* in the incentive approach. We may begin to believe that it would be easy to achieve almost any goal by providing incentives, waving the magic wand of incentive proposals. Indeed, in listening to some of the supporters of incentives, one sometimes has the feeling that they are suggesting that incentives are the magical wrists to direct the invisible hand of the market. The market-place with its automaticity is now to be gently but firmly directed by the incentives decided by government. The best of all possible worlds is thereby obtained: the operation of the market-place in its classical form effectively allocating resources, and the government subtly intervening to make sure that market-place operations achieve government objectives. In this view it is dangerously easy to believe that results will be as intended as problems succumb to the charms of incentives.

What are some of the difficulties in the incentive approach? One question is, of course, will the incentive be large enough to produce the kinds of behaviors which are desired? The more important a behavior to the business or to the consumer, the more must be spent in order to change it in desirable ways. Marginal expenditures may mean marginal returns. There are two effects that follow from these possibilities. One is that the cost of incentives may indeed be very high in order to win the kinds of behaviors that are desirable. Frequently, these costs are overlooked, for they come in the form not of direct expenditures upon the group to be provided an incentive, but as foregone taxes, *i.e.*, taxes that would normally be charged for a particular kind of behavior that are no longer exacted, in order to promote a desired behavior. An incentive to invest in capital goods by reducing taxation on such expenditures can be enormous in terms of taxes foregone. It would be well to have a detailed annual public accounting of taxes foregone in order to provide incentives.

Frequently, a pretended knowledge is utilized. With an exactness that has little basis, predictions are made about how businesses, consumers, and workers will respond to a given incentive. Misleading conclusions can be drawn from this over-confidence in expertise—but, of course, such errors are not restricted to manipulations of incentives.

A second difficulty is that inequities result from providing incentives. Those who are least motivated may have to get the highest return, in order to get them to change their behavior. This may be unfair, because those who willingly change their behavior or already exhibit desired behavior receive less or no rewards for it. And it may be that people similarly situated who should get similar kinds of rewards receive quite differential rewards because of the recalcitrance of one and the amenability of the other.

The inequity question is even broader, since a variety of various kinds of side effects, dysfunctions, and other unintended consequences occur as a result of the efforts to motivate one group or another in the market-place to adopt desired policies. The consequence may be considerably political reluctance to accept the cost and distribution of incentives today.

Another danger is that "incentives" may mask harsh punishments. An example of this is in the 1971 proposals of the New York State Department of Social Services to experiment in two welfare districts in New York City. The welfare benefit would be reduced, and then families would be rewarded for each item of approved behavior that is to be motivated through monetary incentives. Examples of approved, rewardable behavior are getting children to school on time, doing homework, etc. The "brownie point" incentives are already based on an initial and profound punishment—a decline in basic income.

That this kind of "incentive" approach is not an isolated occurrence, at least where poor people are concerned, is revealed in the recent history of proposed legislation about incentives to work for families on welfare. In the mid-sixties, the discussion of welfare, at least by economists and many policy planners, revolved around the fact of disincentives. In the parlance of the time, there was a 100 percent tax on the earnings of welfare recipients, since their welfare benefits would be reduced by the full amount of their earned income. People were thus actively discouraged from working, especially since expenses in working (travel, work clothes, etc.) were not covered by welfare payments. Consequently, the strong recommendation was to lower the tax rate to provide a return for working. Several experiments—the most famous the University of Wisconsin-Mathematica-OEO experiment in New Jersey—were launched to see what responses there would be to different levels of taxation, in addition to basic income guarantee. Despite increasing talk about providing incentives to work, when legislation was drawn up (the Nixon Administration's Family Assistance Plan, which went through many revisions), it not only provided for reduced rates of taxation on earnings of welfare recipients, but it also involved considerable compulsion to work on their part. As Martin Rein pointed out, when the issue became clear, many planners and politicians would not rely on incentives alone to do the job of leading people to work; they wanted *direct* measures, like taking away welfare benefits if adult recipients did not work. The proposed legislation embodied both the incentive of reduced tax rates on earned income and the compulsion of work or training in order to remain eligible for benefits.

Incentives do not avoid political questions; they change the nature of them. Consequently, incentives do not take us out of the market-place of political difficulties; rather, they change some of the issues involved in decision making. When we recognize that incentives are not free goods, but are expenses that could have been used for other purposes, then the question emerges of the comparative returns of various kinds of policies, including those not involving incentives. A companion difficulty may be that the effort to use incentives may make less visible the fact that a policy is being carried out. The result may be to make policy less subject to political control.

The advantages of incentives are high, of course. They try to reconcile the actual operation of policies with their intent. They permit the utilization of individual initiative and provide greater flexibility than do command policies. They are more acceptable policies, at least at their beginning, because they do not push people into actions, but try to engage their self-interest in the operation of a policy. They provide more individual choice than do other policies, and individual choice is a positive phenomenon.

Incentives make sense, since compulsion is a difficult policy to initiate and to utilize effectively in practice. It may be that incentives are becoming popular in part because the U.S.A. is an over-legislated country with an enormous number of laws; we manage to live with this plethora of regulations because

so many are not enforced. Incentives would limit direct legislation of behavior.

The direction of incentives is away from compulsion or regulation and toward influence, whether of consumers or businesses
and even, perhaps, of husbands and wives when demographers
like Kingsley Davis recommend a heavy tax rather than a tax
exemption for each child.

Incentives appear to be a move away from governmental
involvement in the economy, but if they are effective, then
the amount of government activity may increase, for incentives
may be less difficult to utilize politically than overt, active
regulation. The consequence may be less irritation, resentment, and resistance toward an active government.

Incentive policies will undoubtedly increase in the United
States. They can perform some valuable services. But they
are not a magical tool. We should avoid the excessive optimism
about incentives that might lead to premature disappointment
and discarding of them because of unrealized and unrealizable
aspirations. The use of incentives cannot obviate difficult political choices nor ignore powerful and competing interest
groups. The thin line between motivating and controlling or
manipulating people can be easily crossed and yet be
undetected. They can be expensive and produce inequities.
But they can also reduce irrationalities in policies and encourage needed behavior.

They will not end the continuing search for new tools of
policy and planning nor substitute for those currently used.
They are a supplemental tool, albeit a potentially very useful
and flexible one. That should be enough to promote the utilization and study of incentives. If not a panacea, nor are they
a minor improvement.

# Index